To Sue

lots of love

Wendy Page

xxx Go

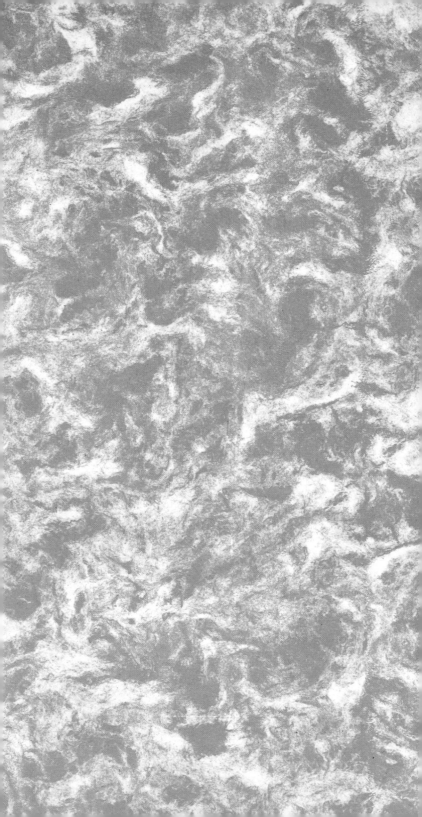

A Miscellany of
CAT LOVERS' WISDOM

A Miscellany of
CAT LOVERS' WISDOM
Kay White

HarperCollins*Publishers*

First published in 1993 by HarperCollins Publishers

Copyright © 1992 by Inklink

A catalogue record for this book is available from the British Library.

ISBN 0 00 412916 4

A Miscellany of Cat Lovers' Wisdom
Compiled by Kay White
Designed & arranged by Simon Jennings
Edited by Peter Leek
Picture research by Ben Jennings
Illustrations & engravings enhanced by Robin Harris

Produced, edited, and designed by Inklink,
Greenwich, London, England
Published in the United States by Running Press,
Philadelphia, Pennsylvania
Typeset in Garamond by Inklink
Printed in Hong Kong by South Sea International Press

A MISCELLANY OF

CAT LOVERS' WISDOM

TABLE OF

CONTENTS

ARRANGED IN SIX CHAPTERS

*"Cats are a mysterious kind of folk,
there is more passing in their minds
than we are aware of."*

SIR WALTER SCOTT (1771-1832)

I N THE 5,000 YEARS SINCE CATS FOUND IT WORTHWHILE *to draw close to the dwellings of man, a great deal has been written about the feline species. And yet some of the world's 200 million cat lovers may feel we are still a long way from understanding exactly how cats think and feel, or why it is that cats are sometimes fickle in giving their affection.*

Cats never tell all they know, and they are seldom completely committed to their owners, no matter how kind they may be. You may own a cat while it is with you, but when it goes out on its mysterious errands, it is a completely independent and self-sufficient animal, always keeping its own counsel. Indeed, some cats maintain more than one home, each household believing that the cat that spends part of the day with them is theirs alone.

Studying a cat's moods, habits, and behaviour is an infinitely rewarding occupation, open to all cat lovers, including those who are housebound or disabled. In these pages you will find all sorts of facts and theories about cats, together with valuable titbits of advice and some fascinating items of feline history. But, inevitably, I have only been able to include a small proportion of the material that has been written about cats during their companionable coexistence with man. I therefore hope this book may encourage others to observe their own cats' behaviour more closely and to explore the rich vein of literature that cats have inspired.

KAY WHITE

DEDICATED TO
"THE BIG CATS"
AND ALL ENDANGERED
SPECIES – LET
WISDOM PREVAIL

CHAPTER ONE
THE LOT OF
THE CAT
IN HISTORY
AND FOLKLORE
A MISCELLANY OF
FACTS & FABLES

THE VERY FIRST CAT

Cats and dogs, and many other flesh-eating mammals such as bears and raccoons, are all descended from a common ancestor.

About 40 million years ago, long before mankind appeared on Earth, a small weasel-like creature known as Miacis thrived in the jungle-like undergrowth and humid tropical climate that prevailed on Earth at that time. Some 20 million years closer to our own era, in the days when dinosaurs roamed the Earth, Cynodictis, a descendant of Miacis, proved to be much more adaptable than its reptilian contemporaries.

From this prehistoric creature, which had such a powerful instinct for survival, are descended the various families of carnivorous animals we know today – including bears, raccoons, weasels, dogs, hyenas, the great cats such as the lion, leopard, tiger, and panther, and the smaller cats such as the easily tamed African wild cat (*Felis silvestris libyca*) and the more ferocious European wild cat (*Felis silvestris silvestris*).

It is the African wild cat that is credited with being the ancestor of *Felis catus*, the modern domestic cat.

WILD CATS

Although *Felis silvestris silvestris* is referred to as the European wild cat, its range extends southward to the savanna grasslands of Africa. Larger than a domestic cat, it has black-striped greyish-yellow fur and a short, blunt-ended tail. North America doesn't have any similar species, but the bobcat (*Felis rufus*) is found in a variety of habitats, from forests to deserts. Many of the world's 37 wild-cat species are now endangered. As a result, the Cat Survival Trust has been established in England to conserve and breed the wild species, and to reintroduce them into places where they have become extinct. In the U.S.A., the International Society for Endangered Cats is concerned with conservation and captive breeding.

Until the 1850s the wild cat was common throughout Britain (it was once quaintly known to naturalists as the "British tiger"), but gradually the entire wild-cat population of England and Wales was killed off by farmers and gamekeepers. However, it still survives in Scotland, where the Highlands, especially around Glencoe, provide an ideal habitat, as well as in a number of other European countries. The strength and ferocity of a cornered wild cat is amazing, although the cats do not attack dogs or man unless provoked. Their usual prey comprises mountain hares, rabbits, and voles, but a large cat can kill lambs and young deer. The cats normally nest among rocks or in the base of hollow trees, but climbers have occasionally seen them in nests deserted by golden eagles.

There are two litters a year, in May and August, usually of four kittens each. The kittens are self-supporting by the time they are five months old. The mother cat has to be very vigilant, as the young cats can be carried off by badgers, foxes, or eagles. Sometimes a wild male will seek out and interbreed with a domestic cat. Once they are two or three weeks old, the kittens become too fierce to handle. Consequently, they are almost impossible to tame unless taken from the nest before their eyes are open and hand-reared in captivity. Even then, the chances of survival are slim, because wild cats have no natural immunity to many of the viral diseases common among domestic cats.

THE FIRST HOUSE CATS

It is thought that in ancient Egypt wild cats tamed themselves by approaching villages where arable farmers lived. The cats made themselves useful by killing rodents, and did not take any food wanted by man. As a result, they gradually became part of household life. Cat bones associated with man were not found until about 1900 B.C. when the opening of a tomb revealed 17 cat skeletons, together with little pots containing dried-up milk.

Cat and Mice.

THE FIRST MOUSERS

By 1000 B.C. cats were serving a valuable purpose in China and Japan. As well as being used to prevent manuscripts in temple and monastery libraries from being eaten by rats, they were employed in the silk industry to keep rats away from the silkworm cocoons.

Throughout Europe, for a long time the usefulness of the cat was less well appreciated. The ancient Greeks had no house cats before about 2000 B.C., ferrets being previously used to control rats and mice. In the rest of Europe, it was as late as the first century A.D. before cats were mentioned in written records. The earliest cat bones found in Britain were dug up by archaeologists on a site dating from the fourth century A.D. at Silchester, in Hampshire. Cats were also brought to Britain by the Vikings, who invaded the country in 800 A.D.

However, cats came to be more greatly valued from the Middle Ages onwards, when rat-borne diseases ravaged Europe and Asia. The worst of these was the Black Death, in the mid fourteenth century, and the bubonic plague, which killed half the population of London in the 1660s.

SACRED CATS

Religious beliefs in ancient Egypt involved a hierarchy of gods and goddesses, some of whom could assume feline form. Male cats were sacred to Ra, the Sun God, who in the guise of a tomcat fought with Apep, the serpent of darkness. Cats and lionesses were associated with the warlike goddess Sekhmet.

Another cat goddess, Bastet, symbolized fertility and motherhood. It is sometimes claimed that the name "pussy" is derived from the Egyptian form of her name. The cult of Bastet reached its height around 950 B.C. Her enormous and extravagantly ornamented temple at Bubastis, East of the Nile Delta, was home to thousands of cats, fed and cared for by the priests night and day. The festival of Bastet in April and May of each year is said to have attracted some 700,000 people, who made the pilgrimage by boat along the Nile to Bubastis.

Around 1000 B.C., a draftsman named Nebra working at the burial site at Thebes had a commemorative stone made. On the stone was a carving of his two sons and an inscription, which read:

"The beautiful cat that endures and endures."

RARE AND EXPENSIVE ANIMALS

Domesticated cats remained exclusive to Africa for several thousand years. When they became important in religious rites in Egypt, no cats were allowed to leave the country – but inevitably some were smuggled out, by Phoenician traders, and sold as rare and expensive animals along the Mediterranean coast. It is believed that the first domestic cat may have arrived in England by jumping ship when a party of Phoenician traders visited the Cornish tin mines.

Cats were also taken to other parts of the globe aboard trading ships and by settlers. Native Americans must have been familiar with cats from quite early times, as their traditional children's games feature dogs and cats on opposing sides. The Avmara tribes of Peru and Bolivia are known to have kept cats, and pet cats were certainly brought to the American continent by settlers from all over the world.

In Egypt, cats were a protected species. To cause the death of a cat, even by accident, was punished by execution. The historian Diodorus Siculus, writing in the first century B.C., records a diplomatic incident between Rome and Egypt which arose from the death of a cat accidentally killed by a Roman soldier.

The Chesnuts from the Fire to draw
The Monkey takes poor Pußies Paw

"A sudden fury and tumult arose, to pacify which, not the ignorance of the miserable wretch, nor any reverence of the Roman name, nor the command of the King himself, who sent the chief of his nobles to appeal for him, was sufficient to save the soldier from being lynched by the indignant crowd."

From THE WONDERS OF THE LITTLE WORLD by REVEREND N. WANLEY, 1678

FELINE FERTILIZER

Egyptian families owned cats as a mark of respect to the gods, and when a cat died the entire household went into mourning.

The cat would be given an elaborate funeral. If the family could afford it, the body was embalmed, then wrapped in a winding sheet decorated with an intricate pattern, usually in two colours. The head of the mummy would be surmounted by a painted linen mask depicting the face of the cat, with the ears fashioned from palm leaves. Then the mummy would be placed inside a jewelled golden casket, and interred in an enormous underground repository containing the remains of thousands of cats.

In 1888, one of these sacred burial grounds was accidentally uncovered by a farmer. An entrepreneur had the bright idea of shipping the remains to England for conversion into fertilizer. One shipload brought 19 tons of mummified bones to Manchester – but few people could bring themselves to use the fertilizer, so the venture failed.

Cat

"The days are long gone by when, to bury a cat, processions of white-robed Egyptians, crowned with convolvulus, acacia and chrysanthemum wound their way with clashing cymbals and the singing of choirs from the temple gates to the sepulchres under the rocks. Now the taxidermist has taken up the duties of the priest, and where the creatures of Pharaohs' adoration used to be spiced, they are now stuffed. They stand in the parlour, and fix with glassy eyes the new tenant of the hearthrug, and from the cold neutrality of wires and wadding, survey the domestic circle of which they once formed part."

From THE LADIES' KENNEL JOURNAL, 1896

DEVILISH BLACK CATS

With the rise and spread of Christianity, the status of cats declined – and black cats came to be associated with Devil worship and witchcraft. Even as late as the nineteenth century it was widely believed that a witch's cat was her "familiar", through which she carried out her evil designs.

Throughout the Middle Ages, cats were persecuted and tortured on feast days in order to drive out the Devil. Anyone encountering a stray cat at night felt obliged to kill it, in the belief that it was a witch in disguise, capable of casting an evil spell on anyone who invoked her displeasure. Many black cats were roasted alive in the company of women convicted of witchcraft, the last of such ordeals being staged in Pennsylvania in 1867.

To dream of a cat is regarded by some folk as a bad omen. It is also said that two cats seen fighting on a grave after a funeral are really the Devil and an angel fighting for possession of the dead person's soul.

The Pufsies when taken are hang'd
Drawn quarter'd beheaded & hang'd.

*"Dream of a black cat at Christmas time
and you will have a serious illness some time
during the next twelve months."*
GERMAN FOLKLORE

GUARDIANS AGAINST EVIL

In the Middle Ages, when plague epidemics or other disasters struck, cats were not infrequently burned alive in the hope that the evil might be averted.

According to a widely believed superstition, sealing up a living cat inside one of the walls was an infallible way of making a building weatherproof. It was also believed that burying a live cat or kitten under the last floorboard of a new house would bring good luck to the occupants; and that burying one in a field before sowing a crop would guarantee an abundant harvest. Less drastically, in Scotland today the family cat is thrown through the doorway of a new house before any member of the family crosses the threshold.

"A black cat put into an infant's cradle will drive away evil spirits."
RUSSIAN FOLKLORE

SHE CATS

Since the earliest times cats have been linked with women, and not always for the most flattering reasons. Ever since the identity of Mut, the great mother goddess of the ancient Egyptians, became merged with that of the cat goddess, Bastet, the female traits of passion, beauty, fertility, and wantonness have been associated with cats. Customarily adulteresses were tied in a sack with a cat and thrown into the Nile, and women who lured men into sexual intercourse were likened to cats stalking mice. The cat's supple movements, its coquettish facial expressions, its teasing habits and covetous eyes all seemed suggestive of seductiveness. Even today, brothels are called "cathouses", and it is usually only women who are accused of being "catty".

THE PRICE OF CATS

In 948 A.D., King Howel the Good of Wales introduced legislation to regulate the price of cats. He ordained that the price should be one penny for a kitten before its eyes were open; twopence from eye-opening until a cat caught its first mouse; and fourpence for a successful hunter. Any person convicted of stealing a good mouser, especially if the cat lived and worked in a granary, was to be fined a milch ewe with lamb and fleece – or, alternatively, as much grain as would cover the cat when suspended by its tail with its head touching the floor.

CATS AND CASH

There are many stories of people bequeathing cash to cats, and not only in modern times. When Sultan El-Daher Beybars died in 1260, he made a bequest stipulating that the produce of an orchard near Cairo should be sold to benefit the starving cats of the city.

More recently, in 1963, Dr. Richard Grier of San Diego, California, bequeathed more than $400,000 to his pet cats "Hellcat" and "Brownie." The cats were quite elderly, and when they both died, two years later, the money was given to George Washington University, in Washington D.C.

However, it would appear that cats can bring humans money, too. A West of Ireland legend has it that cats will give members of a household "a shilling for all they have; fourpence that the housekeeper might be careless and leave the milk out where they could get it; fourpence that they would tread so light that no-one would hear them, and fourpence that they would be able to see in the dark".

SHILLING
British currency unit subdivided into 12 units known as pennies or pence. Shillings and pence were abolished in 1970.

CAT CURES

There are many myths and legends associated with the healing properties of cats. For example, keeping a black cat was said to ward off or cure epilepsy. This may have had something to do with the calming qualities attributed to cats, a virtue still recognized by many physicians today. However, there is no medical evidence to support the following claim:

"Sores on children's eyelids can be cured by passing a black cat's tail over them nine times."
CORNISH FOLKLORE

SAVED BY THE CAT

In the Second World War, during the siege of Leningrad (now once again called St. Petersburg), which lasted 900 days, from September 1941 to January 1944, many of the citizens had no alternative but to eat their pet animals in order to survive. Today, the elderly residents of the city feel they owe their lives to cats and dogs, and to repay the debt many of them will deprive themselves of meat in order to feed pets that have been abandoned by their owners.

OUT OF THE STRONG

There is a delightful, not quite biblical, story about the origin of cats. Noah's Ark was overrun by rats and mice, but the lions were too big to catch them. Noah pondered the problem while stroking the male lion's nose. The lion sneezed, and from his nostrils came forth two small animals, miniatures of the lion but expert mouse hunters. When the Ark came to rest on dry land, it carried an extra pair of animals – the first two cats.

CATS AND THE WEATHER

- If a cat sleeps with its head tucked snugly between its paws, there will be rain.
- If it sleeps with all four paws tucked under its body, the weather will turn cold.
- If the front paws are used to cover the nose, windy weather can be expected.
- If a cat's whiskers droop, there will be rain.
- If its whiskers stick out stiffly, the weather will be fine for a day or two.

RAINING CATS AND DOGS

The expression "raining cats and dogs" is a misunderstanding of the French word *catedupe* – which means a waterfall.

> *"If it rains when a woman puts out the washing, it is an indication that she has ill-treated her cat."*
> GERMAN FOLKLORE

> *"A rainy wedding day means the bride has forgotten to feed her cat."*
> DUTCH FOLKLORE

WEATHER FORECASTING

Cats have always had a strong association with weather forecasting. Many people believe that when a cat rushes about excitedly, tail held stiffly erect and bushy as a bottle brush, bad weather can be expected. A cat that sits washing its face foretells fine sunny weather, but if the washing extends to behind the ears, there will be rain.

> *Careful observers may foretell the hour,*
> *By sure prognostics when to dread a shower;*
> *While rain depends, the pensive cat gives o'er,*
> *Her frolics, and pursues her tail no more .*
>
> JONATHAN SWIFT (1667-1745)

BEFORE THE FLOOD

Before the Cambridgeshire fens of East Anglia were drained, cats were regarded as indispensable for forecasting floods. Every home, no matter how poor, had at least one cat. Several days before the floods came, the cat would try to get upstairs to sleep. If it was prevented, it would choose a sleeping place on top of the highest cupboard. Thus the family were warned of impending high water. Cats were so well thought of that on Sunday they used to accompany the family to church and wait outside during the service. Afterwards they were taken for a short stroll, known as "the cat's walk".

> *"True calendars, as Pussie's eare,*
> *Washt o're, to tell what change is neare."*
>
> ROBERT HERRICK (1591-1674)

SOME CAT WORDS

CAT BURGLAR
A burglar that gets into buildings by climbing up drain-pipes or through inaccessible windows or skylights.

CATBIRDS
Another name for mockingbirds – especially *Dumetella carolinensis*, whose call resembles a cat's mewing.

CATCALL
A shrill whistle or jeer expressing derision.

CATERWAUL
To yowl like a cat on heat.

CATFISH
Fish with barbels (fine spines or bristles) on both sides of the mouth that look like whiskers.

CATGUT
Strong strings made from animal gut (usually sheep's intestines) – traditionally used for stringing musical instruments and sports rackets, and also by surgeons for stitching up wounds.

CATNAP
To doze or have a brief sleep.

CAT'S CRADLE
A popular children's game – you make a cat's cradle (which looks rather like a rope hammock) by looping string between your fingers.

CAT'S-EYE
A reflector set into a small fixture, placed at intervals along roads to indicate traffic lanes at night.

CAT'S PAW
A person lured or inveigled into doing something for another person to further his or her own ends.

CAT'S WHISKER
The wire pointer that made contact with the crystal in early radios, which were known as "crystal sets".

THE CAT'S WHISKERS
Something or someone that's "the best" – the same as "the bee's knees" or "the cat's pyjamas".

CAT SUIT
An all-in-one suit that fits as closely as the skin of a cat.

CATWALK
A narrow walkway (in a factory or other building), or a long, narrow stage used for fashion shows.

KILKENNY CATS

Kilkenny, in Ireland, has acquired a reputation for the ferocity of its cats. To "fight like Kilkenny cats" means to go on fighting till both parties are totally destroyed.

The Prize Fighters

There wanst was two cats in Kilkenny,
Each thought there was one cat too many.
So they quarrel'd and fit,
They scratch'd and they bit,
Till excepting their nails, and the tips of their tails,
Instead of two cats, there warn't any.
TRADITIONAL RHYME

SOME CAT PHRASES AND SAYINGS

ENOUGH TO MAKE A CAT SPEAK
To consume enough alcohol to loosen the tongue. The saying comes from Shakespeare's play *The Tempest*.

ENOUGH TO MAKE A CAT LAUGH
Describes something absolutely ridiculous.

GRINNING LIKE A CHESHIRE CAT
Cheshire cheese (a slightly crumbly white cheese originally made in Cheshire) used to be sold in blocks shaped roughly like a sitting cat. The mysterious Cheshire cat in Lewis Carroll's *Alice in Wonderland* grinned so much it kept on disappearing.

NOT ENOUGH ROOM TO SWING A CAT
This refers to the cat-o'-nine-tails, a whip consisting of nine knotted cords used for floggings aboard sailing ships. Below decks there was barely enough room to swing the whip, which left welts like a cat's scratches.

CAT GAMES

TIPCAT

This was a traditional street game, still popular at the beginning of the twentieth century. The "cat" was a short, sharp-ended piece of wood, which was thrown up and had to be hit with a bat while it was still in the air. From this game comes the saying "Let's see which way the cat jumps." It was no good trying to "tip" the cat (strike it with the tip of your bat) until you could see which way it would fall.

Let them laugh that win.

THE MINISTER'S CAT

This is an old Scottish alphabet game in which each player has to find an adjective to describe the cat belonging to an imaginary clergyman, working through all the letters of the alphabet in turn – for example, "The minister's cat is an agile cat, a bonny cat, a curious cat…" and so on. Any player who is unable to come up with a suitable word goes out. It is a useful game for keeping children amused during boring journeys, but can go on for ever.

G REAT A little a, bouncing B The cat's in the cupboard, and she can't see.

CATS AND MARRIAGE

Cats figure prominently in folklore about marriage. If a girl is in doubt about accepting a proposal of marriage, she should take three hairs from a cat's tail, fold them in a paper, and place it under the steps leading up to her house. Next morning, she must unfold it very carefully to see if the hairs have formed a Y or an N, then give her suitor a "Yes" or "No" as the hairs dictate.

In France, a strange white cat mewing on your doorstep foretells a speedy marriage. In Cornwall, if a bride hears a cat sneeze on her wedding day she will have a happy married life. It is also said that if a single girl treads on a cat's tail she will not marry that year.

The Dog teaching the Cat to Dance

Whenever the cat of the house is black
The lasses of lovers will have no lack.
TRADITIONAL RHYME

FRIGHTENED BY THE CAT

The following strange occurrence was reported at Leiden, in the Netherlands, in 1638:

"A woman of the meaner sort, who lived near the Church of Saint Peter, was delivered of a Child well shaped in every respect, but had the head of a cat. Imagination was that which had given occasion for this Monster, for while she was big she was frightened exceedingly with a Cat which was gotten into her Bed."
From THE WONDERS OF THE LITTLE WORLD by REVEREND N. WANLEY, 1678

SOME CATS OF THE FAMOUS

EDWARD LEAR

Edward Lear's own cat, a large tabby called Foss, inspired his poem "The Owl and the Pussycat."

The Owl and the Pussycat went to sea,
In a beautiful pea-green boat,
They took some honey, and plenty of money,
Wrapped up in a five-pound note.

From THE OWL AND THE PUSSYCAT
by EDWARD LEAR (1812-88)

CHARLES DICKENS

Charles Dickens was very fond of his white cat, William – but was obliged to change its name to Wilhelmina when it produced kittens.

ERNEST HEMINGWAY

At one time, the writer Ernest Hemingway had about 30 cats. He said cats had absolute emotional honesty.

WINSTON CHURCHILL

Winston Churchill had a cat called Nelson during the Second World War. He told his ministers that Nelson did a lot for the war effort – by lying on his feet while he was in bed and acting as a hot-water bottle, thus saving valuable fuel.

DR. JOHNSON

Dr. Samuel Johnson was devoted to his cat Hodge, and used to buy oysters especially for him:

"I shall never forget the indulgence with which he treated Hodge, his cat; for whom he used to go out to buy oysters, lest the servants having that trouble should take a dislike to the poor creature. I am, unluckily, one of those who have an antipathy to a cat, so I am uneasy when in the room with one; and I own, I frequently suffered a good deal from the presence of the same Hodge. I recollect him scrambling up Dr. Johnson's breast, apparently with much satisfaction, while my friend, half smiling and half whistling, rubbed down his back and pulled him by the tail. And when I observed he was a fine cat, saying, 'Why yes, Sir, but I have had cats whom I liked better than this,' and then, as if perceiving Hodge to be out of countenance, adding, 'but he is a very fine cat, a very fine cat indeed.'"

From BOSWELL'S LIFE OF JOHNSON by JAMES BOSWELL (1740-95)

CATS AND THE BRITISH ROYALS

In recent times, royalty has supposedly not favoured cats. Princess Michael of Kent is apparently the exception. She is said to have been devastated with grief when one of her two pet Siamese cats was run over and killed. It is reported that when a supremely regal Siamese cat was presented to Queen Elizabeth II, she quickly gave it away to a footman – who kept it "below stairs" at Buckingham Palace.

Pussycat, pussycat, where have you been?
I've been up to London to see the Queen.
Pussycat, pussycat, what did you there?
I frightened a little mouse under her chair.

From SONGS FOR THE NURSERY, 1805

THE TRUTH ABOUT DICK WHITTINGTON

Richard Whittington, the celebrated Lord Mayor of London, was neither destitute nor friendless as a boy, as legend has it. In reality, he was the son of a well-to-do squire who owned land near the Gloucestershire village of Pauntley. He was born about 1358 and at the age of 13 was sent to London to be apprenticed to a cloth merchant, Sir John Fitz-Warren. According to the legend, Dick Whittington was saved from danger by the cleverness of his cat, who brought him fame and riches. One modern theory maintains that a cat did bring him wealth – but not quite as the legend relates. The true story, it is suggested, was as follows. When Sir John sent a trading ship to Spain, he invited his apprentices to contribute to the cargo. Whittington had heard that, although Spain was infested with rats, cats were rare and fetched high prices – so he sent a cat out on the ship, which was traded for silks, jewels, and ivory. This was the first of many trading ventures, and in later life he always paid tribute to the cat that brought him wealth. The legend tells how Whittington was prevented from leaving London in despair by the chiming of the bells of Bow church, which prophesied that he would become thrice Mayor of London. He did in fact become Mayor three times (in 1396, 1397, and 1406), after marrying Sir John's daughter Alice.

Whittington's Cat destroying the Rats and Mice.

Here lies Richard Whittington, thrice mayor,
and his dear wife, a virtuous loving pair.
Him fortune raised to be beloved and great,
By the adventure only of a cat.

EPITAPH FROM THE TOMB OF RICHARD WHITTINGTON,
DESTROYED IN 1666, DURING THE GREAT FIRE OF LONDON

CHAPTER  TWO

THE HOBBY OF

CAT FANCYING

& SOME FACTS ABOUT FASHIONS

A MISCELLANY OF BREEDS & COLOURS

THE FIRST CAT SHOWS

It was only in Victorian times that cats began to be appreciated for their beauty rather than their ability to catch mice. In 1871, the first cat show was held at the Crystal Palace in London. The opportunity to compete for prizes fostered a much greater interest in pedigrees and cat breeding; and so "cat fancying" was born, in an age when there was keen interest in exhibitions of every kind. The "Cat Exhibition", which attracted 160 entries, led to the founding in 1887 of the National Cat Club – which in 1991 held its ninety-fifth show, with more than 2,000 entries.

Through the patronage of Queen Victoria, who owned a pair of Blue Persians, cat-fancying became a fashionable pastime for aristocratic and well-to-do ladies. Her influence also had an effect on their choice of cats. At the earliest shows, nearly all the cats were short-haired – but by 1896 the long-haired Persian cats were clearly in favour, with 485 entries at the most important event of that year, as against 191 English shorthairs and 64 Siamese. The 740 cats entered at the 1896 show had to stay on display for 22 days. During that time, they were fed 750lb/340kg of minced mutton and 420 pints/238 litres of boiled milk.

In the U.S.A., the first official cat show was held at Madison Square Garden in New York, in 1895.

PRIZE CATS AT THE CRYSTAL PALACE

"Many will remember the sensation created by this first Cat Exhibition, which opened up a channel for the feline race never hitherto dreamed of."
From DOMESTIC AND FANCY CATS, 1895

"A house without a cat, and a well-fed, well-petted and properly revered cat, may be a perfect house, perhaps, but how can it prove its title?"

MARK TWAIN (1835-1910)

IS THERE A CAT IN THE HOUSE?

Australia is the top cat-owning country so far as cats per household is concerned, with 32 percent of the nation's households owning at least one cat. Canada comes next with 27 percent, and the U.S.A. third with 26 percent. In Britain there are at least 7.5 million pet cats owned by 4.6 million households. It is estimated that 31 percent of cat owners have more than one cat. The British spend more on pets than any other European country.

MOGGIES

The term "moggie" is commonly used to mean a non-pedigree cat. Some believe that "moggie" is a corruption of margay, the jungle cat that sailors used to bring back from South America to sell to Liverpool warehouse owners who wished to control rats. Alternatively, Cockney rhyming slang may perhaps have been responsible for the name, "moggie" rhyming with "cat and doggie." Or it may simply be a conflation of "mongrel" and "doggie." A more romantic, if grislier, explanation attributes the origin of the name to a music-hall artiste of the 1890s named Moggie Dowser – who, like many women of the day, wore a wrap round her neck, which looked as if it might have been cat fur.

NEW BREEDS, NEW FASHIONS

There are about 100 pedigree breeds of cat known worldwide, of which about 70 breeds are recognized in the U.K. However, there are more than 300 unofficial breeds throughout the world, and new varieties are constantly being developed – whereas in the world of dogs the last man-made breeds were devised about 100 years ago. A new "designer cat" must breed true for four generations before being accepted for evaluation as a new pedigree breed.

A new breed on the way to being recognized by the Governing Council of the Cat Fancy is the Burmilla, which has its origins in an accidental mating in 1981 between a long-haired male Chinchilla cat and a lilac Burmese female, resulting in four very attractive silver-grey kittens. Intelligent, serious interbreeding has now produced a new dynasty of Asian kittens being developed by a number of breeders.

In America there is a vogue for "leopards for your living room" (i.e. spotted cats), including a breed called Californian Spangles developed by a Hollywood scriptwriter. One of the latest breeds is the Bengal Cat, produced by mating a tabby with a wild Asian leopard cat, then breeding together the friendliest of their descendants. The next fashion may well be for cats significantly larger than the 20-25lb/9-11kg heavyweights that exist today, although cat genetics have not proved easy to exploit in this way. In fact, the largest cat is only four or five times bigger than the smallest – whereas, in the world of dogs, a Great Dane may be 100 times larger than a Chihuahua.

PEDIGREE REGISTERS
There are only two cat-registration authorities in Britain: the Governing Council of the Cat Fancy, and the Cat Association. Cats registered with one authority may not be shown at the events arranged by the other.

WEIGHTY MATTERS

At present, the largest breed is the Ragdoll – an extremely placid cat, with a thickish, slightly ragged-looking coat. Unlike most cats, it becomes almost completely limp when you pick it up. Because it is such a docile animal, it is best not to let a Ragdoll out on its own without a human protector. Although male Ragdolls regularly check in at around 20lb/9kg, ordinary domestic cats can be pretty hefty. In fact, the official feline heavyweight record is held by an Australian tabby named Himmy, who weighed almost 47lb/21kg when he died, aged 10, in 1986.

The smallest breed is the rare, shy Singapura or Singapore Drain Cat (so called because they shelter in drains). Adult females weigh around 4lb/2kg, males about 2lb/1kg more. Although insignificant in size, Singapuras can be valuable.

CAT BREEDS

Some of the most popular cat breeds are described in the pages that follow. There are two extreme body types. The one is essentially the Persian type, which is "cobby" (thickset), broad-shouldered, round-headed, and relatively short-legged, with a thick tail. The other is the lithe, muscular, small-boned, narrow-headed, sleek-tailed body typical of Siamese cats and similar breeds. There are five basic coat types (long-haired, short-haired, curly, wire-haired, and hairless), and a delightful variety of colourings and coat patterns.

SIAMESE CATS

Ownership of these beautiful cats was once confined to the royal family of Siam – but, after several years of persistent diplomatic negotiation, one male and two females reached London in 1886. It is thought that these were the first of the oriental cats to be seen in the West, and that they had been bred for about 200 years before they reached England.

The basic Siamese coat colour is pale cream, but this can only be maintained if the cat is kept in a very warm environment. Originally, the "points" (i.e. the mask, ears, tail, lower legs, and paws) were dark brown. This colour pattern is known as "Seal point". However, during the past 50 years colourings such as Blue point, Chocolate point, and Lilac point have been developed. Siamese cats have an independent, easy-going nature, but they tend to be noisy and assertive, and are often destructive.

BURMESE CATS

The Burmese cat is on its way to replacing the noisy and demanding Siamese as the favourite among the short-haired oriental varieties. It was not until 1948 that the first specimens were imported to Britain from America. They are now almost the most numerous among show cats. Burmese cats are said to have the most doglike behaviour. They are very active, fun-loving animals and are often long-lived. Enthusiastic owners say they make wonderful companions, just like happy children.

ORIENTALS

Orientals have long Siamese-type bodies with a variety of colourings, including tabby and tortoiseshell patterns. They are beautiful, affectionate, gentle and intelligent cats, but also tend to be temperamental and demanding.

ABYSSINIANS

These proud, sleek cats closely resemble the sacred cat of ancient Egypt. Abyssinian cats that have the original ruddy-brown colouring are known as "Usuals". Highly intelligent and extremely devoted, they are bold and love company – but are also very demanding, hating to be ignored or left out of the action.

PERSIANS

Persians are quiet and affectionate, and adapt well to living indoors without access to the outside world. The Colourpoint Persian is a man-made breed. It is a long-haired cat with "Himalayan" (Siamese-type) coloured points, and was first established in the U.S.A. in the 1960s. Colourpoints are extremely placid, but like to be the only cat in the household.

SHORTHAIRS

Short-haired cats tend to be robust and affectionate. They have a solid, compact body and a comparatively large, round head. The fur is dense, though not as thick as a Persian's. There are all sorts of colouring patterns, ranging from black-and-white and plain black to ginger, tortoiseshell, and tabby.

EXOTICS

Essentially an American variety produced by crossing shorthairs, exotics have loads of personality and love other cats and people.

MAINE COON CAT

Thought to be America's oldest breed, the Maine Coon probably evolved from matings between domestic long-haired cats and short-haired cats imported from Asia Minor. It owes its name to its patched, spotted, and striped coat, which resembles a raccoon's. Maine Coons are very hardy, but slow to mature, frequently not reaching full size until they are four years old.

SCOTTISH FOLD CAT

This is the only cat breed that has ears folded down against its head, like those of a dog. It is recognized by the Cat Fanciers' Association in the U.S.A. – but due to fear of spreading impaired hearing and ear disease, it is not recognized by the Governing Council of the Cat Fancy in Britain. A quiet, thoughtful, intelligent, and easy-going breed, it can easily be trained to go for walks, like a dog, wearing a lead and harness.

TAILLESS CATS

The tailless Manx cat is by no means exclusive to the Isle of Man, from which it gets its name. In fact, it seems unlikely that it originated on the Isle of Man itself. A more favoured theory is that one of the vessels of the Spanish Armada foundered on Spanish Rock, close to the island, and several tailless cats that were on board swam to the rock, then continued on to the island at low tide. Joseph Turner (1775-1851), the landscape painter, had seven Manx cats living in his studio, which he said came from the Isle of Man.

Not all Manx cats are completely without a tail. The Isle of Man has an official state cattery to breed Manx cats correctly, as constant tailless to tailless matings result in a lethal gene which means the kittens die before or shortly after birth. Three variations are recognized. The true Rumpie is completely devoid of tail vertebrae. It is rarely healthy, and the kittens often die from spina bifida or persistent diarrhoea. The Rumpie Riser has a few tail vertebrae, which provide it with a vestige of a tail, while the Stumpie possesses a short knobbly or bent tail, and the Longie a somewhat longer, almost normal, appendage.

TAILLESS TALES

From the Isle of Man come stories of a Cat-King who is an ordinary house cat by day but assumes regal status at night. The island's cats are said to be in league with the fairies, who accept them since cats can see ghosts and wraiths. This is why the cat is the only member of the household allowed to stay up when the fairies come into the kitchen at night. If the cat has been put out, then, sure enough, the fairies will let it in again.

FERAL CATS

There are as many as 12 million cats who have either chosen or had little choice but to revert to the semi-wild or feral state. Some have been born into feral colonies and have never lived with humans; others have been abandoned or turned out of their homes; and some have found that domestic life was not to their liking. Cats revert all too easily to a wild state and, once they have done so, quickly become impossible to tame or handle.

Feral cats establish colonies close to a plentiful source of discarded human food, where there is also shelter and warmth. They rarely take up residence in the countryside. Colonies are found around hospitals, airports, docks, factories, warehouses, railway stations, and other urban areas where there are likely to be rich pickings. A colony of dozens or scores of unneutered cats quickly becomes a nuisance. One hospital had to shut its wards when old cats and newly born kittens died within the heating ducts; another found cat fleas pouring out of the ventilators in an operating theatre. Animal charities try to trap these cats humanely and take them to be spayed or castrated so the colony will not increase, but usually only the mildest of the cats can be trapped. It must be said that many people, particularly long-stay hospital patients, get a lot of pleasure from watching these cat colonies – but many more complain of the smell and the noise that the cats make at night.

Poor, little beggar-cat, hollow-eyed and gaunt,
Creeping down the alley-way like a ghost of want,
Kicked and beat by thoughtless boys, bent on cruel play,
What a sorry life you lead whether night or day.
ELLA WHEELER WILCOX (1855-1919)

COATS OF MANY COLOURS

One charity that finds homes for a great many stray or unwanted cats says that blues are by far the easiest to place, followed by gingers, tortoiseshells, and tabbies. In their experience, blacks and black-and-whites are least in demand – despite the fact that black-and-white is the most common colour among non-pedigree cats. Almost any body type can be combined with any coat type, eye colour, and coat pattern or colouring to produce "designer cats", and this is done in all countries where there is a cat fancy.

SOLID-COLOURED
Cats with hair the same colour from tip to root.

BLACK CATS
Most black cats have some white hair somewhere. Usually they have a "locket" under the chin or longer white "guard hairs" dispersed in the coat. A cat that is completely black is not easy to find.

TORTOISESHELL
Tortoiseshell cats, which have an attractive black-and-orange coat pattern, are nearly always female. Contrary to common belief, although rare, tortoiseshell males are not valuable as they are usually sterile.

CALICO CATS
The same is true of calico cats (whose colour pattern is black, orange, and white). The females are extremely fertile, while the males are rare and usually infertile.

VAN OR PIEBALD
These are almost white, but with patches of colour.

BICOLOURED
White with one other colour.

PARTICOLOURED
A coat pattern that includes more than one colour.

HIMALAYAN
The colour of the face mask, ears, legs, and tail contrasts with the colour of the rest of the body. "Himalayan and white" is similar to Himalayan, but with white feet.

TIPPED
"Tipped" means that the tips of the hairs are a different colour from the roots. Cats with lightly tipped coats are known as Chinchillas; medium-tipped cats are classified as Shaded; and heavily tipped ones as Smokes.

TABBY
There are several variations on the "classic" tabby coat pattern, which has three stripes running along the spine and concentric rings on the flanks. "Mackerel" tabbies have parallel vertical stripes on the flanks, and just one stripe running along the spine. A "spotted" tabby coat has a similar pattern, but the parallel lines are broken up by spots.

HOW THE TABBY GOT ITS NAME

The word "tabby" originally meant a silk or taffeta fabric with a watered pattern, the name being derived from the Al-Attabiya quarter of Baghdad, where the weavers of the material worked. In some parts of Britain, a tabby cat used to be called a Cyprus, a name also used for a silk cloth with wavy lines on it.

Tabby Cats.

1210 Tabby Cat Prints. No home complete without a cat. Each half yard of cloth is printed in three pictures. Front, back and feet with outlined margin for cutting. These pictures are to be cut out, sewed together and stuffed with sawdust or cotton, and the result is a life size Maltese tabby, cat in sitting position. The most natural thing of the kind ever produced. Every yard contains two cats. Also have same goods with kittens, 8 to the yard.
Per yard.............$0.13½

HOW THE BIRMAN CAT GOT ITS COLOURS

The first Birman cats were seen in Britain in the mid 1960s. Like Colourpoint Persians, they have a long-haired coat (though not quite as thick as a Persian's) and a "Himalayan" colour pattern. It is said that they acquired their exotic colouring as a result of divine intervention.

Long ago in Burma, so the story goes, white cats guarded the Temple of Lao-Tsun, where there was a gold statue of a goddess, with deep-blue jewels for its eyes. One day, as the head priest was praying before the goddess, with his cat by his side, the temple was attacked by bandits and the priest was killed. The cat placed his paws on his dying master's chest and turned towards the image of the goddess. The next moment, his thick white fur became suffused with gold, his eyes turned a beautiful blue, and his legs, face, and tail changed to a smoky colour, like the colour of earth. Only the tips of his paws, which he had placed on the chest of the dying priest, remained white, as a symbol of his master's purity.

Inspired by this wondrous happening, the other monks gathered up enough courage to attack the raiders, who fled from the temple. When the monks met to choose the head priest's successor, the temple's hundred cats filed into the holy chamber. To the monks' amazement, the cats were no longer white. Their coats were now tinged with gold; the legs, face, and tail of each cat had taken on the colour of earth; and their yellow eyes had changed to a vivid blue. The cats encircled a young monk, who became the new head priest, and the cats retained their special colours – those of the Birman cat we know today.

CAT

CHAPTER THREE

HOW TO CHOOSE
A GOOD KITTEN

A MISCELLANY OF

INTERESTING FACTS

OF CAT LIFE

CHOOSING A KITTEN

Ninety percent of cats kept as household pets are plain, unassuming non-pedigree animals. It is all too easy to be beguiled by the helpless, loveable appeal of a tiny kitten – but it is important to look carefully before you buy one or accept one as a gift. The following guide-lines will help you to make a wise choice:

- Always buy a kitten from the place where it was born – and preferably not from a pet store or rescue shelter, where the kitten may have encountered infectious diseases.
- If possible, buy from a busy household where there are children and a dog too, so that the kitten will have had lots of experiences before leaving home.
- Plenty of affectionate handling and human contact before a kitten is 12 weeks old is crucial to producing a cat with a good temperament for life.
- Do not take a farm cat born in a barn. It will always be semi-wild.
- Ferals, even feral kittens, will never make good pets. They may be impossible to house-train, and they are frequently diseased.
- Do not take a kitten that is too young: 8 to 10 weeks is the minimum age.
- Choose a kitten that looks alert and interested when you play with a moving object.
- The coat should be shiny and glossy, the eyes and ears clean and dry. The kitten should not be sneezing or have any discharge from the nose, nor should it be suffering from diarrhoea.
- Do not choose a kitten whose legs look weak.
- Look for black dust, like coal dust, in the coat. This is flea excreta, and the last thing you want to do is to import fleas into your own home. Once they start to live and breed in your carpets and furnishings, fleas can be very difficult to eradicate.
- Never take on a sickly kitten even as a gift. It could prove very expensive, both in terms of money and heartbreak.
- Don't forget to have your kitten vaccinated.
- Remember that all cats need grooming.

KITTENS GALORE

A Texan tabby called Dusty, born in 1935, gave birth to a total of 420 kittens during her long and productive maternal career. Her last litter, which consisted of just one kitten, was born in 1952. In 1970, a Burmese cat named Tarawood Antigone had a litter of 19 kittens, the largest on record, of which 15 survived. There are normally between five and nine kittens in a litter. The most elderly feline mother on record was delivered of her last litter at the age of 30. When she died, at age 32 in 1989, she had produced more than 200 kittens.

Three little kittens,
Lost their mittens,
And they began to cry.
Oh, Mother dear, we've lost our mittens;
Oh, dear, oh, dear, you silly kittens,
Now you shall have no pie.
NURSERY RHYME

MY PRETTY PUSSY, TELL ME PRAY,
WHERE YOUR THREE COMPANIONS PLAY?
PUZZLE—FIND FOUR KITTENS IN THE ABOVE PICTURE.

MAY KITTENS

There is quite a widespread, though completely unjusti-
fiable, belief throughout Europe that kittens born in
May should not be reared, because they are impossible
to house-train and will bring nothing but sorrow to the
homes that shelter them.

It was the first of May,
My charming little cat,
Deposited six lovely kittens on the mat.
All white May kittens, each with miniature black tails,
Oh, what a lovely chided after such travail.
The cook, dear me, how cruel are our kitchen queens,
Humanity won't mix with cabbages and beans,
She wanted me to drown five kittens out of six.
Five helpless May Day kittens, of all the cruel tricks!
It was not long before they all grew up and thrived,
Below the window of my angry cook at night,
They all lift up their voices, singing with delight.
A year has gone and May Day's here once more,
Six May cats and their Mum have beds on every floor,
And all the seven cats have seven kittens each,
May kittens, white, black tails,
depriving cook of speech.

"MAY KITTENS" by T. WOLDSEN STORM (1817-88)

THE WISDOM OF NEUTERING

When the poem "May Kittens" was written more than a hundred years ago, people were generally not so aware of animal suffering. It is an act of extreme cruelty to try to drown unwanted kittens. A veterinary surgeon will destroy them painlessly.

Charming as this poem is, it also serves to describe very well what can happen when people become overwhelmed with cats. Rescue societies have had to remove as many as 60 cats from one small house from which the owner had been evicted because of the nuisance the cats caused.

Cats are prolific breeders, and many cats are destroyed every year, since owners and animal sanctuaries are unable to cope with the reproductive rate. A female cat can have a first litter when she is less than six months old, and may be well into her next pregnancy before those kittens are weaned. If she is allowed freedom while on heat, she may have kittens by several different sires in the same litter. A fertile female can produce up to 250 kittens in the first 10 years of her life, and still go on breeding until she is 15 years old.

Pet cats of either sex can be neutered early in life to prevent straying, fighting, urine-marking, and kitten production. There is no justification for the theory that a queen should be allowed to have one litter before being spayed. Both toms (male cats) and queens (adult female cats) may be neutered from five months of age until quite late in life, and a queen may be safely spayed when she is well on into pregnancy if she has been accidentally mated.

HOW TO SEX A KITTEN

Sexing kittens and adult cats is not difficult, although mistakes are often made. Female kittens display under their tail a dot (the anus) and a dash (the vagina). Males have two dots, the anus and the external point of the penis. Once the kittens have been sexed, it is a good idea to mark the males behind one ear with a spot of gentian violet (which will eventually fade away), so you know which kittens belong to which sex.

SEX SECRETS OF THE CAT

The mating season starts at the very beginning of the year. Breeders refer to the queen as "calling" when she is on heat. This is an apt term, as the queen can be very vocal at this time. Unlike a female dog, the unspayed queen may "call" constantly for eight months of the year. The queen's typical actions of rolling on the floor, twisting and turning, and yowling loudly, have led many owners to fear their cat is in pain. Not pain, just frustration at being prevented from getting out to meet a male! As female cats return to heat very quickly, it is almost impossible for the ordinary household to prevent a queen from going adventuring, so the decision to have her spayed when young is a very sensible one. Mating between tom and queen is not a joyous occasion – growling, yowling, hissing, scratching, and biting are all routine mating behaviour.

> *Two lady cats, both black and white,*
> *Went on the tiles one Sunday night.*
> *And nine weeks later, sure enough,*
> *They both gave birth to balls of fluff.*
>
> From "MOTHERCRAFT" by MARMADUKE DIXEY, 1936

THE AGONY AND THE ECSTASY

Cat mating almost always ends with the female screeching in pain, and spitting and hissing at the male. This is because the male cat has barbs on its penis that permit smooth entry but stab with real pain on withdrawal. The pain is supposed to stimulate hormonal activity that causes an egg to be released for fertilization.

PREGNANCY AND BIRTH

Pregnancy lasts about 63 days, so the first kittens of the year are born in early March and will be ready to go to new homes 10 weeks later. Kittens should not be taken away from their mother earlier than this, as they have a lot to learn from her before they are ready to go out into the world.

Mating finishes in May or June, with the last litters of the year being born in August. Between midsummer and the following January there is little mating activity, so there is always a scarcity of young kittens between late fall and early spring.

PUSSY WILLOW

The pussy willow legend is attributed to Poland. A mother cat is said to have mewed so piteously when her kittens were thrown into the river that the willow trees along the bank bent down their branches for the kittens to cling to. And since that day, every spring, the willow has grown buds that look and feel like cat fur.

MOTHERLY LOVE

Dams (mother cats) often move their kittens, when they are a few days old, from the nest in which they were born to another location. This is a security measure, to prevent predators finding the kittens while the mother is out hunting. The tiny kittens are carried, one at a time, by the loose skin at the back of their necks. The dam will often return to the first nest after she has moved all the kittens. Scientists have deduced from this that the cat does not always know how many kittens she has.

"About ten days ago one of my cats (whom I shall call Number 1) had five kittens, of which I drowned four. Yesterday another cat of mine (a descendant of the first cat mentioned) also had five kittens, and soon after they were born cat Number 1 discovered them, and started taking them into her own bed and suckling them. Number 2 cat, not to be outdone in the matter of motherly duty, took them back again to where they were born. And so they were carried backwards and forwards all day until I made a bed large enough for them all, when both cats lay down together, caring for the kittens indiscriminately, the kitten first born looking like a giant to the others."

Reader's letter from THE COUNTRYSIDE MAGAZINE, 1905

CALLING YOUR KITTEN

Use your cat's name when it comes to eat, and while you are stroking it. Call the cat only when it is about to come to you anyway. Do not call it to you soon after it has eaten, or as it is settling down to sleep. You will just be teaching it that it's perfectly all right to ignore your wishes. Smokey, Sooty, and Fluffy appear high in the league of popular names, followed by Tigger, Tinker, and Timmy. More unusual, though also popular, are Gismo, Pudding, Amber, Mittens, Motley, Bertie, Belle, and Toffy. Dairymaid is a country name for a tortoise-shell cat. Tib-cat refers to a female, hence the pet names Tibbles and Tibby. Felix and Sylvester, the cartoon cats, are named for their wild forebear *Felix silvestris* – while Tom, of Tom and Jerry, is just an ordinary tom cat.

Our old cat has kittens three,
What do you think their names should be?
One is tabby with emerald eyes,
And a tail that's long and slender.
And into a temper she quickly flies,
If you ever by chance offend her.
Now, don't you think that Pepperpot
Is a nice name for a cat?

One is black with a frill of white,
And her feet are all white fur.
If you stroke her she carries her tail upright,
And quickly begins to purr.
Don't you think that Sootikin
Is a nice name for a cat?

One is tortoiseshell, yellow and black,
With plenty of white about him.
If you tease him he at once sets up his back,
He's a quarrelsome one, ne'er doubt him.
Don't you think that Scratchaway
Is a nice name for a cat?

"CHOOSING THEIR NAMES" by THOMAS HOOD (1799-1845)

TWO'S COMPANY

Owners who are out for the greater part of the day may want to consider getting two kittens, so they can keep each other company and play together – which helps to develop intelligence and body skills. If you are going to buy two kittens, it is best to get them at the same time, as they will settle in better than if one kitten is bought first and then another arrives later.

CURIOSITY KILLED THE KITTEN

Kittens face all sorts of hazards, even within the security of the home, as a result of their natural curiosity. The following are commonly reported danger zones:

FRIDGES
Make sure your kitten has not crept inside before you close the door of your refrigerator or freezer. If such an accident occurs, warm the kitten slowly. Don't feed the kitten while it is chilled; and don't give it alcohol.

CUPBOARDS
Check cupboards before closing them. A cat can do a great deal of damage if it goes to sleep inside a glass or china cupboard and then wakes up in the dark. Be particularly careful not to let your cat into a cupboard containing cleaning materials.

CANS
Flatten all cans that have contained food, so your cat doesn't get its head stuck inside one should it decide to explore your dustbin.

DOORS
Before closing a door, always make sure that your cat is clear of it and hasn't suddenly decided to squeeze past you. Many cats, especially kittens, sustain severe tail or body injuries through being squashed by doors.

NOOKS AND CRANNIES
When house repairs are in progress, check very carefully before replacing the last floorboard or piece of panelling. New places to explore have an irresistible fascination for cats, and they often get trapped inside.

CHAPTER  FOUR

A LITTLE TREASURY OF

CAT BEHAVIOUR

& SOME GOOD
ADVICE ON HOW
TO COMPREHEND IT

CATS' EYES

Cats have a reputation for being able to see in the dark. Although no animal can see without some light, it is true that cats have much better night-time vision than humans do, owing to the position and construction of their eyes. The reason why cats' eyes shine in the dark is that the pupils are wide open at night – so the back of the eyeball reflects light from a torch or car headlight.

"A veterinary hospital in Suffolk has just restored the sight of a cat which was almost totally blind, following ulceration of the eyes. Under a full anaesthetic the abnormal tissue in the eyes was cut away and purpose-made contact lenses were inserted in the eyes while the tissue healed. After twelve days the contact lenses were removed and the cat could see again."

From THE ANIMAL HEALTH TRUST REPORT, 1992

HEARING

Cats have much more acute hearing than either humans or dogs. However, white cats with blue eyes are often deaf, which is an inherited trait. If a white cat has one blue and one orange eye – a feature permitted in the showing world – then the cat may be deaf in just one ear. Since cats are able to walk with supreme confidence along branches, fences, and roof tops, the balancing mechanism in their ears must be particularly effective. For this reason, cats, unlike dogs, hardly ever suffer from travel sickness.

A SNIFFY EXPRESSION

Cats grimace after they have sniffed at certain smells. This is because, like horses, cats have an additional scent organ situated in the roof of the mouth. Using this organ, a cat will approach the source to be investigated with its head held still and its lips partially retracted in what looks like a sneering expression. The grimace (known by the German word *Flehmen*) is held for a second or two, then the cat will carefully lick its nose. This procedure is most often used for analyzing the urine or other excretions of other cats.

SPITTING WITH FURY

Spitting is commonly used as a demonstration of anger and threat of aggression, which in the animal world is often the most effective means of defence. At the same time, to make itself look even more threatening, the cat usually arches its back and raises its fur.

LAYING A SCENT

Cats, especially males, mark the boundaries of their territory by spraying urine or making scratches on posts. The urine sprayed is thought to vary according to the cat's purpose. For example, the urine sprayed before a fight is more pungent than the urine passed as normal body waste – and the smell of urine sprayed in order to punish its owner is different again.

Spraying is not the same as passing urine in a normal manner. It is performed from a standing position, with the cat facing away from the object that is to be marked. Standing a few inches away from it, with tail upright and quivering at the tip, the cat will aim a few short spurts of urine backward at its target.

Spraying can be triggered by the introduction of a new pet into the home, or a new baby or unfamiliar adult, or even something as apparently innocuous as new carpets or furniture. To the cat, all these things may seem to threaten its security.

THE OFFENDED CAT

Cats take offence easily. Any invasion, any alteration on its territory or emotional upset, and a cat is likely to use one of its potent range of weapons against its owner – scratching the furniture or ripping off wallpaper, defecating on the owner's possessions or on the owner's bed, or, worst of all, spraying. Both males and females, regardless of whether or not they have been neutered, will turn to spraying when they want to reimpose their dominance upon their territory.

DISCOURAGING SPRAYING

If a cat sprays in just one place, strips of aluminum foil strewn around the offending area may keep it away from the spot it has chosen for spraying. Feeding the cat close to where it has sprayed and sprinkling some dried food around the area may also act as a deterrent, as cats do not like to eat where they have sprayed and the desire for food is likely to win.

CLEANING UP SPRAY

Cat urine is corrosive, persistent, and extremely pungent. However, if you use ammonia or chlorine bleach to clean it away, that compounds the smell and the cat will respray in the same area again and again. A more effective remedy is to clean the sprayed object with a 10 percent solution of washing powder recommended for removing biological stains, or with a proprietary cleaner available from vets and pet stores. Then rinse thoroughly with cold water and wipe or spray with rubbing alcohol, which should also be worked into any crevices in floorboards etc.

PREVENTING SCRATCHED FURNITURE

Cats don't like the smell of oranges. Susie Page, a well-known writer on cat subjects, therefore recommends pinning pieces of fresh orange peel onto upholstered furniture where your cat sharpens its claws. Renew the orange peel as it dries.

FOILING THE CAT

Cats hate anything sticky on their feet, so the same writer suggests spreading syrup all over your kitchen work surfaces to prevent Tom-and-Jerry antics while you are out of the house. True, you will come home to sticky work surfaces and you will have sticky paw prints all over the floor and work surfaces, too. However, if you repeat the process for a few days, you should find that the cat stops using your work surfaces as a sleeping place or territory for uninhibited exploration. Covering your work surfaces with aluminium foil is an alternative deterrent, as cats don't like the crackling noise it makes when they walk on it. Aluminium foil can also be used to keep your cat off your cooker or stop it walking on polished table tops.

If you have an electric cooker that has on and off buttons flush with the surface, it is advisable to turn the cooker off at the main switch when you leave the house – as it is all too easy for an animal to press the buttons, causing a burner to become red-hot, which may start a fire.

FELINE DELINQUENTS

Prevention is better than punishment, since cats tend to associate punishment with the person who inflicts it rather than with their own behaviour. Nor is it possible to train a cat to obey you – since cats, unlike dogs, do not strive to please. So all you can do is use strategy or guile to prevent or deter the cat from doing things you don't want it to do – e.g., by shutting vulnerable possessions away in cupboards and keeping house-plants in hanging baskets. The following are some useful tips for dealing with anti-social feline behaviour. Any reprimand must be administered within a minute or two of the offending act being committed.

JETS OF WATER
You can squirt water at the cat as it is performing or is just about to perform the action you want to curb. Cats dislike this, but don't link the deterrent with the perpetrator. A water pistol or a plant spray containing pure clean water can be used, or a garden hose outdoors.

WELL-AIMED MISSILES
Alternatively, if your aim is good, you can throw a bean bag or small cushion toward (but not directly at) the cat. But don't let the cat hear or see you handle the thrown object, or it may mistrust you forever after.

NOISY DETERRENTS
Smacking has little deterrent value – and you stand little chance of catching the culprit! Shouting "no" may be more effective, but the cat may ignore you for a long time afterwards or become nervous and withdrawn.

The careless Servant leaves the Dish, While Puss in Pattens steals a Fish

RUBBING

Cats very frequently rub their faces and bodies against objects or other animals, and against people too. The patches between the ears and eyes, the lips, the chin, and the tail are all supplied with glands that produce fatty secretions. When your cat rubs against you and other members of the household, it is marking you as part of its family – or at least indicating that you all belong to the same gang.

"It is generally supposed that cats are more attached to places than to individuals, but this is an error. They obstinately cling to certain places, because it is there they expect to see the persons to whom they are attached. A cat will return to an empty house, and remain in it many weeks. But when at last she finds that the family does not return, she strays away, and if she chances then to find the family, she will abide with them."
From ENQUIRE WITHIN UPON EVERYTHING, 1877

NOSE TO TAIL

A cat uses the tip of its nose to distinguish between hot and cold. Its whiskers, which are used for judging the space around its head, are extremely sensitive and should never be touched or pulled. A stiffly raised tail is a sign of friendliness to other cats and to humans – but when it waves its tail, that is a sign of displeasure.

HOW MANY BONES?

Cats have 230 bones in their skeletons, 25 more than man. The shoulder construction is very loose so that a cat can turn its head round over its back, which is useful for grooming and allows it to see behind. Normal cats have five toes on their front feet and four on their hind feet, but to find paws equipped with one or more extra toes is not uncommon.

AN ESSENTIAL TOOL

A cat's tongue is rough so it is able to lick the bones of its prey clean, and also to provide an excellent tool for grooming. Loose hair is pulled out by the rasps on the tongue, which point backward down the throat, allowing the cat to swallow the hair that has been removed during grooming. Balls of hair swallowed in this way can accumulate in the stomach, causing discomfort. Eating grass, either outdoors or from a tray of grass grown indoors specifically for this purpose (see page 93), will help the cat to bring them up.

CLEANLINESS

Many people believe that cats are very clean animals because they bury their faeces. However, they do not always do so. Feral cats usually leave their faeces exposed in piles, and cats wandering outside their home area will also leave faeces uncovered. Cats will often cover up left-over food, even scratching on a tiled floor in an effort to do so. Typically, this action is used when the food is not much liked.

USING THE HOUSE AS A TOILET

If your cat is passing urine or faeces around the house, first consider whether you have done something to upset the cat, since very often this particular behaviour pattern is used to express dismay or as a protest about changes in the household. If your cat is spraying in the house, get your vet to check the cat in case there is some physical reason, such as cystitis or arthritis, that is causing it to spray. Otherwise, since spraying of this kind is an almost compulsive act, the only effective remedy is to identify the reason why the cat feels the urge to spray. If the cat is depositing faeces in secluded corners around the house, try to establish why the cat is disinclined to use its litter tray, bearing in mind the following questions:

- Is your cat's litter tray sufficiently private? If it isn't, make a "hood" for it from a cardboard box.
- Is it large enough? Long-haired cats, in particular, generally prefer a spacious litter tray.
- Is it too close to the cat's eating or sleeping places?
- Have you changed the type of litter recently? Some cats find certain textures or deodorants unpleasant.
- Has the cat become allergic to the litter? Some types of litter contain dust particles that irritate the throat.
- Do you clean out the litter tray often enough? Your cat's litter tray needs to be cleaned out every day.
- Has the cat found a surface that it prefers, such as a particular carpet? If so, try lining the litter tray with offcuts of carpet for a time, and see whether the cat starts using its litter tray again.

Never, never "rub its nose in it". This disgusting and spiteful act of revenge does no good at all and is likely to make the cat deeply distrustful of its owner. In fact, the cat may become so nervous that it won't come near the owner and may even keep away from the house.

KNEADING

Cats will habitually stand on their owner's lap and knead or press with their front paws, often with claws extended. Besides being quite painful, this also tends to ruin your clothes as threads of cloth are likely to be ripped out. Although owners regard this kneading gesture as a sign of affection, it is noticeable that cats often choose to inflict it on complete strangers who are not particularly keen on cats. The visitor then has to pretend to be honoured by the cat's attention.

PURRING

Cats have the very particular ability to purr – as a sign of contentment, enjoyment, and affection for their owners. Kittens can purr from their earliest days, and a cat will purr contentedly when it is entirely alone. However, it has been noticed that cats purr almost constantly when they are incubating feline flu. They also sometimes purr when they are frightened or threatened, or as a sign of submission.

The purr is thought to originate in the larynx and to be produced by rapid vibration of the cat's vocal cords. Purring is sometimes described as "singing the thrums" (a kind of repetitive humming or strumming), perhaps because it is often accompanied by paddling of the feet, with claws extended.

Anthropologists believe that if an ancient language lacked a word for "purr", the people who spoke the language did not keep cats as pets. This would appear to be true of the ancient Greeks and Romans.

THE CAT.

CAT LANGUAGE

Once you have established a good relationship with your cat, you will have no trouble understanding what your cat is saying to you or what it wants done. Communication the other way is not so easy, and your cat is quite likely to ignore your wishes.

Meow, the cat's most frequently used sound, can be voiced in many ways – for instance, it can be *me*-ow or me-*ow*. Scientists have identified some 16 different sounds in the cat's repertoire, each sound being used for a different purpose by individual cats. Each of the sounds is accompanied by a specific demonstration of body language, mainly the way the cat's ears and tail are held and the way its eyes change, but sometimes the whole walk alters to aid expression of an emotion. A happy cat going to greet its owner will have its tail stiffly raised and its ears pricked up. The eyes will be narrowed and the cat may blink, to express affection. Many cats make a special chirruping sound, rather like a bird call, as a sign of welcome to the owner.

A cat defending its home or its territory dilates the pupils of its eyes so that they look solid black, and its ears are held in the horizontal position. The cat may hiss menacingly and curl its lips into a snarl, with the erector muscles in its coat all working to bush out the fur in order to make the cat look larger and more formidable than it really is. An even angrier cat will growl deeply in its throat, with its ears held low on the face and pulled back, while the bushed-out tail is held low and moves furiously. Tooth chattering is a signal of angry frustration, most often made when a cat can see its prey, usually a bird, very close but cannot reach it. Among the many other cat communication sounds are the mew (made with the lips almost closed) and the silent meow, a pleading gesture, when the lips open but no sound comes out.

Siamese cats are undoubtedly the most vocal breed, particularly when the female is on heat. She may yowl at a piercing level, almost constantly day and night, for days on end. No less strident is the caterwauling of two ordinary tom cats fighting over the right to mate a female, an eerie sound that haunts the night hours.

MONKEY BUSINESS

Cats are excellent tree climbers on the way up, using their front claws to grip the bark and their hind-leg muscles to push the body up. Coming down is not so easy, as the hind claws are not designed to grip at this angle. An experienced cat overcomes the problem by climbing down trees backward.

There's no need to panic when you see a cat apparently stuck up a tree, mewing pitifully. Left to its own devices, the cat will generally work out the best way to get down.

MAD HALF-HOURS

Cats are often described as having "mad half-hours" – usually in the early evening – when they rush around the house, up and down curtains, and over the furniture. This is thought to be a throwback to ancestral behaviour, as twilight would be the most active hunting time in the wild. This type of behaviour tends to gradually diminish as the cat gets older. Similar frenzied behaviour on windy days is also thought to be due to the "call of the wild".

"He will kill mice and will be kind to Babes when he is in the house, just as long as they do not pull his tail too hard. But when he has done that, and between times, and when the moon gets up and night comes, he is the Cat that walks by himself, and all places are alike to him. Then he goes out to the Wet Wild Woods or up the Wet Wild Trees or on the Wet Wild Roofs, waving his wild tail and walking by his wild lone."

From JUST SO STORIES by RUDYARD KIPLING, 1902

SWIMMING CATS

It is not true that all cats shun water. In fact, although they don't often swim, cats are sometimes seen swimming across shallow rivers in order to hunt on the opposite bank. The Turkish Van Cat, first imported from the Van Lake area of Turkey in the 1950s, is notoriously fond of swimming and playing in water.

"A friend of mine recently has a cat which was certainly not afraid of the water. It would come in several times a week soaking wet and its owner could not understand this until one day he noticed puss swimming across the River Soar making for home. It crossed the river after the rats and rabbits in a small spinney, and after a time was missing, having undoubtedly paid the penalty of his poaching propensity by falling a victim to the gun of the gamekeeper."
Reader's letter from THE COUNTRYSIDE MAGAZINE, 1905

TEXTILE SUCKING

It used to be only wool, especially cashmere, that cats liked to suck and eat, but now all sorts of textiles go the same way. At one time this habit was confined to the Siamese breed; but now, possibly as a result of inter-breeding, other breeds and non-pedigree cats, too, have developed this dangerous and expensive habit. One animal behaviourist recommends that textiles should be rinsed in a weak solution of quinine to make them unpalatable. Menthol and eucalyptus oil have a similar effect. Wool sucking may indicate a return to infantile behaviour, as the smell of wet wool may remind the cat of the moist fur around its mother's nipples.

GROOMING

It is a fallacy that cats can keep themselves clean. An adult long-haired cat may require as much as an hour's grooming a day, and even then in a centrally heated home it will shed hair throughout the year. Show cats have to be bathed regularly, and lesser cats may need washing sometimes. Cats often signal embarrassment by having an impromptu wash and brush up.

"Why do cats wash after a meal? A cat once caught a sparrow and was about to eat it, when the sparrow said: 'No gentleman eats until he has washed his face.' The cat was impressed and set the sparrow down so that he could wash, but the sparrow flew away. This annoyed the cat so much that he vowed, as long as I live I will eat first and wash afterwards."
From "THE CAT AND THE SPARROW" by JEAN DE LA FONTAINE (1621-95)

DIGGING IN THE GARDEN

If your cat starts digging in your garden, reach for your hose and squirt it with water from a distance, so it will not link you with the deterrent (see page 56). Dusting the soil with pepper or proprietary repellents generally has little effect, but fine plastic netting is useful for covering seed beds. If your cat digs in a nearby garden, give your neighbours permission to use the hose on it (if need be, more vigorously than you would at home) and tactfully advise them not to pet or feed the cat, or otherwise encourage it to visit their property.

CHAPTER  FIVE

HUNTING & FEEDING

AN INSIGHT INTO

CAT APPETITES

A MISCELLANY OF

FEEDING HABITS

CAT THE HUNTER

Even the best-fed pet cats will hunt, because hunting is their natural behaviour. Indoor cats generally have to be content with hunting spiders and flies, whereas outdoor cats have a much wider range of prey available to them. Many pet cats never catch anything, but they still go through the ritual of stalking. The skill of a first-class hunter has to be learnt as a kitten, and practiced frequently thereafter.

One cat who had clearly paid attention to her stalking lessons was Towser, a champion mouser owned by a distillery in Scotland, who died in 1987. It is estimated that during her working life she caught more than 28,000 mice, averaging at least three a day.

A CAT'S MIXED BAG

"When I was a boy we had a cat, a great hunter, and she brought home most of her 'bag'. A weasel was nothing uncommon, and I have seen her bring in a hare, swung over her shoulder, as big as herself. On one occasion she brought home two partridges, carrying them both at the same time. But the most wonderful 'catch' of all was a live trout. One night at the 'back end', when the trout were 'on the run', she brought home one eight inches long. It was put into a basin of water, where it swam about. In less than ten minutes after, puss had another one the same size, and it, too, was alive. Both trout were returned to the stream the next morning alive and well."

Reader's letter from THE COUNTRYSIDE MAGAZINE, 1905

Now, truly, saith Sir Cat.
I know how sparrows taste by that,
Exquisite, tender, delicate.
This thought soon sealed the other's fate,
But hence what moral can I bring?
For lacking that important thing,
a fable lacks its finishing.

JEAN DE LA FONTAINE (1621-95)

STALKING AND STAKE-OUT

A cat will hunt by stalking prey across a field or in the garden. Once a rodent's burrow has been identified, the cat will ambush the exit until one of the inmates emerges. Cats watch these holes with an amazing degree of concentration, fixing their gaze not directly upon the exit but at a slight angle, as the cat's sight is keenest at the edge of its visual field. A cat may steadfastly watch a burrow for well over an hour before it has the opportunity to pounce on a small rodent.

Take a cat and foster him well with milk
And tender meat, and make his couch of silk,
But let him see a mouse go by the wall,
He will abandon milk and meat and all,
And every dainty that is in the house,
Such is his appetite to eat a mouse.

From THE CANTERBURY TALES by GEOFFREY CHAUCER (c.1340-1400)

THE PREY

Mice and young rats are the cat's favourite prey. Moles and shrews are seldom eaten, as they have glands on the side of the body that emit a nasty smell and taste. Nevertheless, these animals are hunted and sometimes brought back home, since cats cannot resist anything small that moves, even grass snakes, lizards, and frogs.

Not all cats are able to hunt birds successfully. Catching a bird is in fact no mean feat, as the cat has to leap into the air to pounce on the bird and cannot follow the prey if the first attempt fails, as it can with a mouse that is trying to escape.

Blackbirds are often caught and eaten, whereas house sparrows, which are comparatively easy to catch, apparently make cats vomit. In a fable by La Fontaine, a cat and a sparrow set up house together, but another sparrow flies in and threatens the cat's friend. The cat kills and eats the invading sparrow, but it tastes so good that he decides to eat his friend too. Perhaps the sparrow was a dunnock (hedge sparrow), which cats do find good to eat.

THE KILLING BITE

The killing bite of a cat is very precise. It is targeted on the spinal cord of its prey, and the cat's sharp, pointed front teeth have to enter between two neck vertebrae in order to sever the spinal cord and bring instantaneous death. A cat always eats its prey with the head pointing down its throat, so the fur or feathers will go down smoothly. Victorian nursery rhymes and stories often characterize cats as having a sly, deceitful nature and a killer instinct – unlike dogs, which are nearly always portrayed as noble and self-sacrificing.

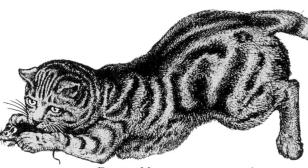

Doctor Mouse came creeping,
Creeping to her bed,
Lanced her gums and felt her pulse,
Whispered she was dead …

Old Mother Tabbyskins,
Saying, serves him right,
Gobbled up the doctor,
With infinite delight.

From MOTHER TABBYSKINS WAS ILL AND SENT FOR DR. MOUSE

BOY EATS CAT

"A country lad, about sixteen, for a trifling wager, ate at a public house in this town, a leg of mutton which weighed near eight pounds, besides a large quantity of bread, carrots, etc. The next night, the cormorant devoured a whole cat smothered with onions."

From THE CAMBRIDGE CHRONICLE, ENGLAND, 1770

THE CAT WHO CAME TO DINNER

A sculpture of a cat named Kaspar is kept at London's Savoy Hotel for a very special purpose. Whenever there's a dinner party of thirteen, if the guests are concerned about the superstition that the first person to leave the table will be the first to die, Kaspar is invited to make the party up to fourteen. The statue is then duly seated at the table, with a napkin tied round his neck, and the whole dinner is served to him, together with the other guests.

NO TO VEGETARIANISM

Cats don't thrive on a vegetarian diet, for two reasons. First, they lack many of the enzymes needed to digest vegetable material. Secondly, taurine (a derivative of cysteine, one of the amino acids), which is absolutely essential to cats, is found in meat but not in foods of vegetable origin. Lack of taurine can lead to blindness.

DAINTY EATERS

A cat's stomach is small in relation to its weight, which is why cats need two or three small meals a day. Automatic feeding bowls are now available that allow a cat access to food at preset times when the owner is out.

THE VALUE OF FUR AND FEATHERS

A cat living on a natural diet of mice and other rodents enjoys quite varied nutrition, as it devours them whole, consuming the fur, intestines, and stomach content of its prey, as well as the muscle meat. If you feed your cat only fine steak and little else, you therefore deny it a lot of essential vitamins and minerals, which you must then provide as supplements, in the form of tablets and powders.

HOLD THE LIVER

Although cats like liver, only a very small amount should be given as a treat once a week. An excess of liver can result in severe bone disease.

AND THE FISH

Contrary to popular belief, cats are not natural fish eaters. A diet of nothing but canned fish may cause painful inflammation of the tissues, and a diet of raw fish can lead to a deficiency of Vitamin B.

The hapless nymph with wonder saw,
A whisker first and then a claw.
With many an ardent wish,
She stretched in vain to reach the prize.
What female heart can gold despise,
What Cat's averse to fish?

From "ODE ON THE DEATH OF A FAVOURITE CAT" by
THOMAS GRAY (1716-71)

SERVING YOUR CAT

Feed your cat from a flat plate rather than a bowl. Cats do not like getting food on their chins, and they find it annoying to have their whiskers touching the sides of a bowl. Avoid placing the food plate and water bowl close to the litter tray – cats naturally find this arrangement distasteful. Cats generally like their food served at blood heat and prefer it to be moist. Meat chunks in jelly is one of their favorite foods. Many cats like to eat little and often – but once food has become dry and stale, a cat has to be very hungry before it will eat it.

CONVENIENCE FOODS

Not surprisingly, 90 percent of cat owners find it easiest to feed their cats on commercially prepared canned cat foods that are carefully balanced for optimum nutrition, including all the necessary vitamins and minerals. Cats should never be fed dog food. Although it may be slightly cheaper, it is quite different in formulation and may contain preservatives that are harmful to cats. Cats do appreciate a variety of flavours in their diet, which is why the selection of cat food occupies so much shelf space in supermarkets. Many cats enjoy nibbling at biscuit-style dried cat foods – but if your cat consumes a great deal of this type of food, then make sure that it drinks plenty of water.

DRINKS FOR CATS

Cats don't actually need milk, although some are very fond of it. In fact, drinking milk or cream to excess can bring on diarrhoea, so make sure your cat always has fresh water available and only give it milk as a treat. Although its bowl is regularly filled with fresh water from the kitchen tap, you may notice that your cat prefers water with other flavours and likes to drink from puddles or a dripping tap in the yard, or even from the bowl of the toilet. You should therefore never leave buckets containing disinfectant or plant fertilizers, or other harmful substances, where your cat can get at them, in case it is tempted to sample the contents.

The cat is grown small and thin with desire,
Transformed into a creeping lust for milk.
A long dim ecstasy holds her life,
Her world is an infinite shapeless white,
Till her tongue has curled the last holy drop,
Then she sinks back into the night.

From "MILK FOR THE CAT" by HAROLD MUNRO (1879-1932)

A CAT'S COMRADESHIP

"Two cats, not related, were recently missed for several days from their home village, and have just been accidentally found in a loft, one with its foot in a trap, and the other sitting beside it. The floor was littered with the remains of dead mice, birds, etc., which the one not trapped had evidently brought up to feed its imprisoned friend, and it had not even left its companion long enough to go home to rest."

Reader's letter from THE COUNTRYSIDE MAGAZINE, 1905

LUXURIOUS TASTES

Many cats relish luxuries such as smoked salmon and cod's roe, avocados, asparagus, and certain fruits. Less predictably perhaps, some cats adore chocolate, crisps, peanuts, and even cheese.

"There are more ways of killing a cat than choking her with cream."
From WESTWARD HO! by CHARLES KINGSLEY (1819-75)

FASTIDIOUS AS A CAT

Cats are fastidious creatures, with a highly developed sense of smell and taste. Although attracted by strong-smelling foods, cats won't touch putrid meat; and if they can't smell because of an infection, will refuse to eat.

THE CAT-MEAT MAN

Early this century, before canned pet food was available, there was a thriving door-to-door trade in cat's meat. The vendor pushed a cart, or rode on the back of one pulled as often as not by a depressed-looking pony. Lumps of cooked and dried horse meat were proffered on skewers to housewives alerted by the cry of "Cat's meat, cat's meat!".

SHOCKING BEHAVIOUR

Some cats have a passion for chewing cables. This can be fatal to the cat – and to the owner, too, if the cat's action causes a fire. As a preventative measure, paint the cables with eucalyptus oil to make them unpalatable, and unplug your electric appliances when not in use. Like wool sucking, this type of chewing probably reflects boredom and may cease if the cat has more outdoor activity.

CHAPTER 🐈 SIX

CARING FOR

YOUR CAT

A MISCELLANY OF INFORMATION ON CAT EQUIPMENT, HEALTH & WELL-BEING

LIVING WITH A CAT

Living with a cat is a partnership of give and take. Very often there is rather more "give" on the owner's side, but owning a cat can be a source of great pleasure to both of you if you observe the following rules:

- Cats are happiest with a regular routine and expect meals to be served on time.
- Keep your cat's drinking bowl filled with water.
- Don't leave your cat out at night. Always check that it is in before you go to bed.
- Don't treat your cat as if it was a small dog. Cats become alienated if you try to train them or demand dog-like obedience from them.
- Unless you want kittens, have your cat neutered so it won't be distressed by mating urges it can't fulfil.
- If there are other animals or small children in the house, give your cat a high place where it can sleep undisturbed. A cushion on top of a cupboard makes an ideal refuge and viewing point.
- Consult a qualified vet if your cat seems ill. Never let anyone but a vet put down unwanted kittens.
- Follow your vet's advice about vaccinations, and don't forget when boosters are due.
- Cats enjoy company, and kittens enjoy being played with. Spend time with your cat, talk to it, and let it get accustomed to being handled so you can help it if it is in trouble. But always remember that your cat has a life of its own.

TRANSPORTING YOUR CAT

The first essential when you acquire a cat is a carrying cage, which will be useful throughout your cat's life. Wickerwork baskets are less practical, and you should never trust a cardboard box with string tied round it. Buy a cage made of plastic-covered wire. One with a top that opens is more convenient than a cage with flaps at each end, as it is easier to lift the cat out.

LITTER TRAYS

Even if your cat is going to be allowed outside in the daytime, it will need a litter tray to use as a toilet overnight. Open shallow ones are cheap; but some people, and some cats, prefer a litter tray with a hood over it, which affords a greater degree of privacy. Whichever type you buy, make sure it is large enough for the cat to sit in comfortably. Remember to clean out the litter tray every day.

Garden soil or sand used to be the normal filling for litter trays, but nowadays pet stores offer a variety of different types of litter, some of which contain deodorants. Cats will often show a marked preference for a particular kind of litter and may refuse to use the one you have bought – so be prepared to experiment with different types until you find one your cat approves of.

Today cat litter is a multi-million-pound business, as it is now much more common for cats to be kept indoors all the time.

Monkey & his Cat

HANDLING LITTER TRAYS

Always wear protective gloves when handling your cat's litter tray. This is especially important for women who are or may become pregnant. There is a parasite called toxoplasma that takes up residence in cats' bowels and lays its eggs in the faeces. Contact with the eggs can result in humans becoming infected by the parasite, which may cause women to abort. Dogs can become infected if they swallow the eggs, and bitches may lose their puppies due to the infection.

PROTECTING YOUR PLANTS

If you want to protect plants in window boxes, or in containers on your patio or inside the house, cover the surface of the compost with large pebbles so the cat won't use it as a toilet.

BEDS FOR CATS

There are two favourite types of cat bed. One is a hammock that can be slung from a radiator, which is total bliss for a heat-loving cat. The other is just an ordinary cardboard box, like the ones you bring the groceries home in. Nevertheless, it's true that a cat will sleep anywhere, and cats love boxes of every kind.

SCRATCHING POSTS

Cats have an instinctive desire to sharpen and clean their claws. They do so by scratching energetically on a variety of surfaces, and tend to have a preference for your best antique table or nicest armchair. You can buy scratching posts, usually cardboard cylinders covered with carpet, from pet stores. But it is easy to make your own by nailing a piece of carpet to a board, preferably in such a way that both textures can be used. Attach the scratching board or post to a wall, so the cat can really pull on it. Elaborate posts that extend from floor to ceiling, incorporating boxes at different levels, give indoor cats exercise and amusement – in effect, providing a tree in your living room.

TOYS FOR CATS

Cats must have something to play with indoors. Anything that moves can be a plaything for a cat. A ball of crumpled paper or a balloon is great fun; so is a bunch of feathers dangled from a flexible stick or a pair of tights tied in a knot, but best of all is a large paper bag (never give your cat a plastic one). A toy that cats find quite intoxicating, and gives them exquisite pleasure, is a piece of cloth tightly stuffed with the leaves of *Nepeta cataria*. This blue-flowered plant, popularly known as catnip or catmint, is easy to grow outdoors. If your neighbours grow it, be warned: their border is sure to be devastated by your cat rolling ecstatically on the plants. On some cats, the herb valerian (*Valeriana officinalis*) has a similarly intoxicating effect.

COLLARS FOR CATS

Every cat should wear an elasticized collar bearing its owner's name, address, and telephone number. Even cats kept indoors all the time sometimes escape. It is advisable to have your vet's name, address, and phone number on the identity tag, as well. Sometimes people finding an injured cat are reluctant to take it to a vet in case they become liable for the cost of treatment.

BELLING THE CAT

"Long ago, the mice held a general council to consider what measures they could take to outwit their enemy the cat. A young mouse got up and said:

'You will agree that our chief danger consists in the sly way the enemy approaches us. Now if only we had some signal of her approach! I propose therefore that a small bell be procured and attached round the neck of the cat, then we shall always know when she is about.'

This proposal met with general applause until an old mouse said: 'That is all very well, but who is to bell the cat?' Nobody spoke. Then the old mouse said: 'It is easy to propose impossible remedies.'"

From THE FABLES OF ÆSOP by JOSEPH JACOBS, 1894

WALKING THE CAT

Siamese and Burmese cats take most readily to wearing a body harness and walking on a lead, if trained to do so from kittenhood. Even so, it is more a case of the owner following the cat than the cat going where the owner wishes. Lead walking is particularly useful if you are holidaying, so your cat can enjoy browsing in new surroundings safely.

IN AND OUT

Cats are no longer put out at night. Not only is the practice regarded as cruel to the cat, it is also unfair to neighbours who have to put up with the noise of caterwauling and cat fights. A survey among cat owners reveals that about 25 percent of their cats live very happily and healthily indoors all the time, and are never allowed outside at all. According to the survey, those cats which are allowed free access to the outside world stay out for only two to six hours each day.

Scientist Sir Isaac Newton is credited with inventing the cat door – a small hinged flap fitted near the bottom of a back or side door, which allows the cat to go in and out without the door having to be opened. Cat doors are a great boon to cats and owners alike, provided they are small enough not to be a security risk.

WHY DO CATS HAVE NINE LIVES?

The number nine has been associated with cats from time immemorial. According to French folklore, in Brittany there is a *chat d'argent* (a "money cat") that can serve nine masters and make all of them rich. The number nine has also always been associated with spells and witchcraft.

In a more modern context, some cats regularly dodge death by a hair's breadth, especially under the wheels of passing vehicles. However, many others do not survive their first encounter with machinery and other products of technology. Present-day hazards include sewing needles with thread attached, burners and hotplates on kitchen cookers, chewing electric flex, falling from high buildings, eating plastic bags or toys, drinking anti-freeze, eating anti-slug pellets, eating grass treated with weedkiller, eating birds poisoned by agricultural chemicals, and, above all, being knocked down or run over by traffic. In the home, washing machines and spin dryers are particularly dangerous. The combined attraction of warmth, human clothing, and things that go round and round can prove irresistible. A curious cat may climb into the machine – and if it is not checked before switching on, the consequences can be fatal.

BITTER MEDICINE

Veterinary fees can amount to hundreds of pounds for surgery following an accident or for treating a persistent skin disease or digestive problem. Insurance that covers the cost of veterinary fees is therefore a prudent and extremely worthwhile investment.

"Good king of cats, nothing but one of your nine lives."
From ROMEO AND JULIET by WILLIAM SHAKESPEARE (1564-1616)

HAVING YOUR CAT VACCINATED

Do not hesitate to have your kitten vaccinated against infectious diseases. Many of the most dangerous feline infections are passed from cat to cat by sneezing, so vaccination is well worthwhile. Even if your cat never meets another feline, you can bring viruses home on your clothes. All good boarding catteries, and all cat shows, ask to see up-to-date vaccination certificates. Telephone your nearest veterinary surgeon to find out about the best vaccination programme. For pedigree kittens, it should begin before they leave the breeder.

A LIFE-SAVING VACCINE

A new vaccine designed to protect cats against feline leukemia may eventually lead to the development of a vaccine that will conquer AIDS in humans.

Professors Oswald and William Jarrett, two veterinary surgeon brothers working at Glasgow University Veterinary School, in Scotland, have discovered that the feline AIDS virus behaves in much the same manner as the human variety. The University of California has already made two types of experimental vaccine for cats, and researchers report that the results are encouraging. It is not inconceivable that in the future, thanks to this work with cats, it may be possible to vaccinate humans against AIDS. In the meantime, it is reassuring to know that feline AIDS is not infectious to humans.

Sadly, up till now feline leukemia has often been a killer disease. Hundreds of thousands of pet cats carry the leukemia virus, and around 30 percent of them die within three years of showing symptoms.

THE CAT'S DEADLY ENEMY

Today, the car is the cat's most deadly enemy. Cats tend to be oblivious to the dangers of traffic, in the city as well as in rural areas, and frequently dice with death when crossing roads. Also, because they enjoy warmth, cats like to sit underneath cars or even right inside the engine compartment – so always check that there is not a cat squatting under your vehicle, or sitting behind or in front of it, before you drive away.

If you come across a cat that has been injured by traffic, take it as quickly as possible to a veterinary surgeon for diagnosis and treatment. Unless you are a qualified veterinary surgeon, do not attempt to do more than render first aid yourself. The following tips may be useful if you should encounter an injured cat:

- Take the injured cat out of the line of traffic before it is hit again. Watch the traffic constantly as you do so – you may be almost invisible to motorists, especially to anyone driving a high-sided vehicle, while you are bending over the cat.
- A cat in pain will take revenge on anyone who comes near it – so wear leather gloves, and avoid putting your face close to the cat.
- Try to locate and contact the victim's owner. Since cats are territorial animals, it is likely that the injured animal's home may be nearby.
- Take the cat to a veterinary surgery. There is little point in calling a vet to the site of the accident, and veterinary call-out charges can be high.
- Wrap the cat tightly in a large towel or rug, with its limbs close to its body. If the cat is badly injured, lift it on a board (or even a shovel, if the victim is a small cat or kitten) to avoid causing pain.
- Injured cats do not bleed as freely as dogs do, since they have fewer major blood vessels close to the surface of the body.
- When taking the victim to a veterinary surgeon or back to its owner, place the cat in a secure carrier. Alternatively, if the journey is short, confine the injured cat to the boot of the car, in case it recovers en route and attacks the driver or tries to escape.

A CAT WITH TEN LIVES

In the churchyard of St. Mary Redcliffe in Bristol, there is a stone dedicated to a cat who fell victim to a car in an age when the streets were quieter. The inscription reads:

TO THE CHURCH CAT 1912-1927
Here lies the body of Tabby Tim,
An enormous family mourns for him,
Ten lives he had and would have had eleven,
If he hadn't got in front of an Austin Seven.

AUSTIN SEVEN
A small family car made in Britain during the 1920s and 1930s.

CAT BITES

Studies at the University of California have shown that cat bites, even quite small ones, on humans are much more likely to become infected than the more sinister-looking bite of a dog, as the wound inflicted by a cat's teeth tends to be deeper and is therefore more difficult to disinfect. As a result, up to half of all cat bites need immediate hospital treatment and the administration of antibiotics. Older patients, particularly those suffering from osteoarthritis and immuno-suppressive diseases, are at highest risk. Research suggests that infection is most likely to occur in people over the age of 50 and, in all age groups, when bites are on the hands.

HOW TO GIVE TABLETS TO A CAT

Never give a cat a tablet while it is occupied in other ways – especially when using its litter tray, as that may deter it from ever using a litter tray again. Giving tablets to a cat is never an easy operation, but it can be accomplished if you act quickly and gently. The most effective procedure is as follows:

- Wrap a large towel round the cat to confine its limbs.
- Place your first finger and thumb alongside the cat's whiskers, and your third and fourth fingers behind the ears. The cat's head can then be tilted back, and its mouth will open automatically.
- Use your other hand or a pair of blunt forceps to place the tablet on the back of the tongue. Blow gently into the cat's face and stroke its throat in a downward direction to encourage swallowing.
- Watch for the cat to open its mouth and lick its lips, otherwise it may just be pretending to take the pill.

DANGEROUS DRUGS

Never give a cat aspirin, not even children's aspirin, as aspirin is extremely poisonous to cats. Never give a cat any form of tranquilizer without first taking veterinary advice. Some tranquilizers and travel tablets make cats more excited, not less.

ORAL HYGIENE

Cats suffer a great deal if they have even a slight pain in their mouths. They become depressed, and will refuse to eat or drink because of comparatively mild tooth or gum problems. Many pet cats will tolerate having their teeth brushed with a soft toothbrush to prevent build-up of plaque.

POISONING AND HOW TO AVOID IT

Cats are particularly vulnerable to poisoning by common substances, since they cannot metabolize certain drugs and chemicals. They are especially sensitive to disinfectants containing carbolic, and by licking their paws or coat often ingest poisonous materials that they would not deliberately eat.

A surprising number of garden and house plants are poisonous to cats. Among the most common ones are buttercups, clematis, crocuses, foxgloves, hyacinths, hydrangeas, larkspur, and lily of the valley, as well as mistletoe and various other berries. If you are growing any of these plants indoors, put them into hanging baskets so your cat cannot get at them.

Certain plant foods, as well as fungicides and insecticides and other garden sprays, can poison cats – so make sure surplus water does not remain in saucers or other containers in which plants stand, in case it is contaminated by chemicals or plant food.

VENOMOUS BRAINS

"The flesh of cats can seldom be free of poison, by reason of their daily food, eating rats, mice, wrens and other birds which feed on poison: and above all the brain of a cat is most venomous, for it being above all measure dry, stoppeth the animal spirits, by reason whereof memory faileth, and the infected person falleth into a frenzy. In Spain and Gallia Narbonense [southern France] they eat cats, but first of all take away their head and tail, and hang the flesh a night or two in the open air to exhale the poison of it, then finding the flesh to be almost as sweet as a cony."

From HISTORY OF FOUR-FOOTED BEASTS by EDWARD TOPSELL, 1607

A CRUEL EXPERIMENT

Cats have often been exploited in the cause of the advancement of science, a practice that unfortunately continues to the present day. The following account, by a Captain Hall from South Carolina, U.S.A., describes the effects of rattlesnake poison on animals and tells how an innocent cat fell victim to a cruel experiment in the colony more than 250 years ago:

"We thought his [the snake's] poison was not spent; so we got a cat (for we could get no more dogs) which he bit about an hour after, though I can't say where. The cat was very sick and we put her in a closet: by some means she was let out in less than an hour and a half after she was bitten. The next morning early she was found dead in the garden and much swollen; so that nobody cared to examine or search where she was bit."

Some time later Captain Hall reported that his fellow citizens were not too happy with his experiments on the animals of the neighbourhood:

"Dogs and cats were not to be had; for the good women whose dogs had been killed exclaimed so much that I durst not meddle with one afterwards."

From EXPERIMENTS ON THE EFFECTS OF THE POISON OF THE RATTLE-SNAKE by CAPTAIN HALL, South Carolina, 10 May 1720

DECLAWING

When cats destroy furniture or curtains, the removal of their front claws is often discussed. However, this mutilation should only be used as a last resort – and never on a cat that spends some time out of the house, since without front claws it can't defend itself from attack. Recourse to declawing is more frequent in America than in other parts of the world. In fact, many vets are very reluctant to perform the operation, believing that, besides deforming the paws, it can result in severe mental depression. However, artificial "soft" claws are now being fitted to avoid this sense of deprivation.

THE WILL TO SURVIVE

In 1950, *The Times* newspaper received a report that a four-month-old kitten had followed a party of climbers to the very top of the Matterhorn, in the Alps. In 1964, another brave cat, a two-year-old tabby, survived being trapped in a lift shaft for 52 days without food or water. Whilst it may not be true that cats are blessed with nine lives, some seem to have an unfailing ability to extricate themselves from perilous situations. Others display remarkable stamina or tenacity, as witness the following account of feline endurance:

"One of the most remarkable facts I ever came across in regard to the tenacity of the life of any animal was in the case of a large tabby cat of mine. He was once worried by a dog when sitting on our own doorstep and we never saw him again for three weeks, although we sought for him all over the district. After the absence of three weeks he turned up one Sunday morning and could scarcely crawl in. We gave him food and milk, and (astounding and almost unbelievable though it seems) the milk which he was drinking was slowly trickling to the floor from a hole in his stomach. On examining him we found quite a large rent in the under part of his body which must have been torn by the dog three weeks before, but where he had been and how he had existed baffles me. However, the wound healed up in about four days and he lived hale and hearty for a year or two after this."

Reader's letter from THE COUNTRYSIDE MAGAZINE, 1905

SIGNS OF ILL HEALTH

Apart from eating grass, which seems to ease feelings of bloat or indigestion, cats do not do anything to cure themselves when they are ill – beyond perhaps refusing food and drink and, if they are seriously ill, hiding in a secluded place ready to die. Generalized signs of illness are sometimes seen in the eyes – especially when the third eyelid, which is not normally visible, appears to be drawn up, partially obscuring the eye.

Mouth ulcers, bad breath, and failure to eat, a "staring" (spiky) coat, discharge from the nose, laboured breath, diarrhoea, and straining on the litter tray, whether to urinate or pass faeces, are all sufficient reasons for seeking veterinary advice. A sick cat can deteriorate very quickly and may be infecting other cats in the neighbourhood, so do not delay getting help.

It is important for owners to check their cats once a week, so any signs of illness or injury can be detected at an early stage, while they are easier (and cheaper) to treat. When your cat is on your lap, check for lumps, cat-bite abscesses, and any painful areas on its body and limbs. Check the coat for flea excreta – a coal-black dust in the fur that turns red when wetted, which is the remains of a flea's meal of blood.

DEALING WITH FLEAS

When you find evidence of fleas, treat all the cats, dogs, carpets, and upholstery in the house immediately, as the warmth of modern houses makes them ideal breeding grounds for fleas. If treatment is neglected, a massive infestation could result – and animal fleas *do* bite humans. Get flea-eradication treatments from a vet, as many products on sale are poisonous to cats.

CAT TO CAT

A great many feline diseases are caused by viruses that are easily passed from one cat to another. Among the viral diseases are cat flu, infectious enteritis (feline panleucopenia), feline leukemia, and feline infectious peritonitis. Some of these diseases cause the cat to shed virus particles capable of infecting other cats for a long time after the original victim has recovered.

CAT TO HUMANS AND BACK

Some diseases can be passed from cats to humans, but humans can infect their pets, too.

TUBERCULOSIS AND HUMAN INFLUENZA
Both these diseases can be passed to cats by humans.

MUMPS
Cats may develop enlarged glands in the neck as a result of picking up mumps from children.

SALMONELLA
Sometimes a whole household, including pets, is stricken by food poisoning, either due to the cat bringing home infected prey or because poor-quality pet meat has been prepared in the kitchen and knives or cutting boards have transmitted the bacteria to human food.

RINGWORM
This fungal infection, which often produces itchy "rings" on the skin, is transmissible from cats to humans.

RABIES
Although not endemic in all countries, rabies is the most serious disease that animals can transmit to man.

TOXOPLASMOSIS
This infection, which can be contracted from cat faeces, is dangerous to pregnant women since it may cause abortion or fetal deformity (see page 78).

KEEPING YOUR CAT CLEAN

Kittens learn how to clean themselves by copying their mother, and they are usually completely skilled in this routine by the time they are six weeks old. Every cat washes in exactly the same way. The face is cleaned first, using the back of one paw and the lower part of the front leg dampened with saliva. This cleansing routine takes care of the face, the chin, and around and behind the ears. Then each hind leg is held in the air (an action sometimes called "playing the banjo") while the saliva-laden tongue goes over the whole body except for the spine, which the cat cannot reach.

Some people believe that a cat bathed against its wishes will never wash itself again. But this is quite untrue, and elderly or arthritic cats, cats that have been ill, and cats that have rolled in fox droppings will need human assistance with their ablutions. Plan to bathe the cat in the sink, in a warm room with windows and doors closed. Line the bottom of the sink with a folded towel, and lay another towel on a nearby flat surface ready for when the cat is lifted out of the sink. Use tepid water and a shampoo specifically formulated for cats – even the most luxurious human shampoo is unsuitable for cats, as is any perfumed shampoo.

Make a "collar" from a length of cotton cloth to help you grip the cat. Wear strong household gloves to avoid being scratched and bitten. If the cat objects strongly to being bathed, make a bag out of towelling with a drawstring around the neck, so the cat can be put into the bag, then lowered into the water and bathed while inside the bag. Dry the cat with warm towels, and keep it indoors for several hours. Most cats will not tolerate being dried with a hair dryer.

White cats look better for a dry shampoo. Use an unperfumed proprietary formulation and make sure to brush it all out. Dark-coloured cats may be treated similarly, using bran slightly warmed in the oven. Cats shed dead hair when subjected to stress. A visit to the vet may make your cat moult all over the examination table. Brushing and combing a short-haired cat, then "polishing" it with an old pure-silk head square, helps to remove loose hair and so prevents hairballs.

GREENERY FOR HEALTH

Always have some trays of grass or sprouting seeds available for a cat that is kept indoors or lacks access to grass, as cats make use of grass as a laxative and as an emetic. Cocksfoot grass (*Dactylis glomerata*) is the type they like best. As already mentioned, hairballs swallowed during grooming can accumulate in the stomach, which causes discomfort, and eating grass helps the cat to bring them up. If a blade of grass is swallowed whole and is not digested, it may protrude from the rectum after the cat has had a bowel movement. This can cause the cat a great deal of distress, so the blade of grass should be grasped with a tissue and gently extracted. While doing this, wear household gloves, which must then be thrown away.

A CAT NAMED TRIPOD

If a cat is knocked down by a car or caught in a trap, it is sometimes necessary for the vet to amputate a badly injured limb. In a recent issue of *The Feline Advisory Bureau Journal*, a veterinary nurse recounted the story of a cat named Tripod, or Trip for short. Within a day or two of having his right foreleg amputated, Trip was using his litter tray, balancing on three legs – hence his name. Within days of the operation Trip adapted his walk to a bunny-hop, and within months could scramble up trees. However, not surprisingly, he needed help with washing his right ear and the right side of his face.

FELINE HIGH-RISE SYNDROME

There is a charming story about the Prophet Mohammed's cat, Muezza. One day the Prophet found the cat asleep on the sleeve of his robe. Rather than disturb her, he cut off the sleeve. On his return, Muezza got up and bowed to him three times. The Prophet then stroked her three times down the length of her back. According to Islamic tradition, this gave cats their ability to land on their feet when they fall from a height.

However, this blessing does not always work, or at least not entirely. "Feline high-rise syndrome" is the modern veterinary term used to describe the injuries cats receive when they sky-dive from buildings two stories or more high. The cats sometimes survive leaping from amazing heights, the most common injuries sustained being to chest, face, chin, and limbs.

In 1965, it was reported that a cat fell (or leapt?) 120 feet/36.6 metres from an eleventh-story balcony and walked away unharmed and unperturbed.

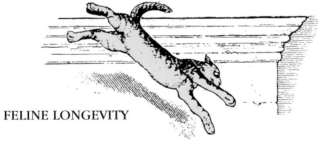

FELINE LONGEVITY

Cats are considered to be elderly when they are over 12 years old. Siamese cats live longest, and Chinchillas tend to be comparatively short-lived. The American Feline Society received a report of a cat in Hazleton, Pennsylvania, that had reached the age of 37; and there have certainly been quite a few other instances of cats that have lived to 30 and over.

So far as the average unneutered domestic cat is concerned, provided they are healthy and well looked after, males generally have a life span of 13 to 15 years, while the average female life span is 15 to 17. Neutered cats tend to live a year or two longer than cats that have not been neutered. Many cats live to 14, although by then they are usually beginning to feel their age.

PAINLESS AND PEACEFUL

There is no easy way to cope with the heartache when a pet cat has to be destroyed. It is the price we pay for loving. The way a pet is 'put to sleep' (given euthanasia) is exactly the same as when a cat has a general anaesthetic. The vet injects an overdose of a strong anaesthetic into a vein in the front leg. Your pet falls into a deep sleep, and within a few seconds all the body's systems have ceased to function and your pet is dead. It is all painless and very peaceful.

HOW OLD IS YOUR CAT?

A comparison between human and animal ages used to be arrived at by multiplying the animal's age by seven, but this formula has now been superseded.

A more accurate calculation is to assume that a one-year-old cat is equivalent to a 20-year-old human (since a cat aged one is fully adult and capable of breeding), then after its first birthday to treat each cat year as being equal to four human years. This makes a 10-year-old cat the equivalent of a 56-year-old human.

Another theory treats a cat aged one as being 15 in human terms; a cat aged two as 25; a cat of four as 40; a cat of 10 as 60; a cat of 15 as 75; and a 20-year-old cat as being the equivalent of a human aged 105.

If I lost my little cat, I would be sad without it,
I should ask St. Jerome what to do about it,
I should ask St. Jerome, just because of that,
He's the only Saint I know that kept a pussycat.

The author and publishers
gratefully acknowledge the following:

Cat World (monthly journal)
Cats (weekly journal)
Feline Advisory Bureau Journal
Journal of Small Animal Practice

Animal Health Newsletter, College of Veterinary Medicine,
Cornell University, August 1991
The Animal Health Trust Report, 1992
Art for Commerce, Scolar Press 1973
Buffon's Natural History, Milner & Company 1868
The Cat Care Manual, Bradley Viner, Quarto 1987
Cat Psychology, R. H. Smythe, TFH Publications
The Cat Repair Handbook, H. Loxton, Macdonald 1985
Catlopaedia, J. M. Evans & Kay White, Henston 1988
Cats Ancient and Modern, F. C. Sillar & R. M. Meyler, Studio Vista 1966
Comic and Curious Cats, Angela Carter, Gollancz 1979
Complete Cat Book, Anna & Michael Sproule, Multimedia Publications 1985
The Countryside Magazine, 1905
The Curious Cat, Michael Allaby & Peter Crawford, Michael Joseph 1982
Do Cats Need Shrinks?, Peter Neville, Sidgwick & Jackson 1990
The Domestic Cat, D. C. Turner & P. Bateson, Cambridge University Press 1988
The Dover Pictorial Archive Series
The Encyclopaedia of Illustrations, Studio Editions 1990
Enquire Within Upon Everything, Houlston & Sons 1877
The Everlasting Cat, Muriel Kirk, Faber 1977
"Experiments on the Effects of the Poison of the Rattle-snake" by Captain Hall,
from *Philosophical Transactions for the Years 1720-32,* London 1733
Fables, J. Gay, C. Whittingham 1801
The Fables of Aesop, Joseph Jacobs, Macmillan 1894
(reprinted by Godfrey Cave 1979)
The Guinness Book of Records (1970 & 1992 editions), Guinness 1970 & 1992
The History of Four-footed Beasts, Edward Topsell, 1607
Images of World Architecture, Bonanza Books 1990
Let's Talk Cats, Susie Page, The Stephen Greene Press, Vermont 1980
The Poetry of Cats, ed. Samuel Carr, Batsford 1974
Sir Richard Whittington, Walter Besant & James Rice, Chatto & Windus 1905
Standard Guide to Cat Breeds, Grace Pond & Ivor Raleigh, Macmillan 1979
Understanding Your Cat, Michael Fox, Blond & Briggs1974
The Victorian Catalogue of Household Goods, Studio Editions 1991
The Wonders of the Little World, Rev. N. Wanley, London 1678
Woman at Home, George Newnes 1912
Words, Beasts & Fishes, Marmaduke Dixey, Faber 1936
You and Your Vet (article by Alison Hudd), 1992
Young Folk's Companion, J. Erskine Clarke, George Sully 1894

*"Cat said, I am not a friend and I am not a servant.
I am the cat who walks by himself and
I wish to come into your cave."*

From JUST SO STORIES by RUDYARD KIPLING, 1902